'This is a brilliant, timely book for everyone – especially when life is vulnerable and volatile – and it has been written by one of the most resilient leaders I know.'
Pete Greig, 24-7 Prayer International and Emmaus Rd Church

'Patrick and I have been close friends for many years. Over that time I have seen him experience some extraordinary challenges, not least extreme surgery to both legs and the resulting physical and emotional scars. What makes Patrick uniquely qualified to write this book is not just his wisdom on resilience but also the fact that he has so much lived experience of bouncing forward. He is an absolute inspiration to me and I know that you are going to find this book utterly life-giving and a support to anyone who is walking through a challenging season of life.'
Rev Will Van Der Hart, Co-Director of mindandsoulfoundation.org

'Without a triumphalist platitude in sight, Patrick offers a gentle yet compelling invitation to resilience. Like all good magpies, he has masterfully woven together nuggets of spiritual treasure from an impressive array of wise teachers, but it's his own authentic wisdom that stands out the most. I loved this practical book and came away feeling encouraged and hopeful again – and so will you.'
Tanya Marlow, pastoral theologian and author of *Those Who Wait*

'Shot through with remarkable honesty, deep hope and the kind of authentic wisdom only ever gained through lived experience, this is a book for our times.'
John Sutherland, former Met Police Borough Commander and author of *Blue* and *Crossing the Line*

'This is essential reading for all humans. Patrick's research and reflections are deeply personal but universal to our experience. The way he explores how we build resilience in our lives is really practical, immensely inspiring and so helpful. I'm sure something in this book will resonate and make a difference for you, as it has for me.'
Abby Guinness, Head of Spring Harvest Programme

'This book is a must. Not just because we are living in unusually difficult times, but because there's no sense that difficult times will ever cease to be present, this side of heaven. In *Bouncing Forwards*, Patrick draws on a rich tapestry of sources, stories, facts and figures to help us build our resilience and ability to navigate the rough terrain of our lives. He writes with both passion and compassion to draw us forwards into growth, into courage and ultimately into a deep sense of peace that is not dependent on our circumstances, but is shaped by who we are on the inside.'
Arianna Walker, CEO of Mercy UK

'Nobody is immune from the storms of life, and Patrick's book is a lifeboat while the waves are crashing. But it is much more than that: *Bouncing Forwards* is a guide that helps us to navigate through tricky waters so that we become better equipped for the journey of life. It's an honest, wise and practical handbook for growing in resilience. I can't recommend it highly enough.'
Cathy Madavan, speaker, broadcaster and author of *Irrepressible: 12 Principles for a Courageous, Resilient and Fulfilling Life*

'Once again, Patrick is disarmingly honest and powerfully vulnerable. *Bouncing Forwards* reminds us that our stories are not ended by failure or vulnerability, and that grace and hope are the strongest antidotes to despair. This book renews the soul, soothes the heart and reminds us that it is OK not to be OK.'
Rev Malcolm J. Duncan, pastor, author, faith and social policy advisor, broadcaster, theologian, international speaker

'It's been said that good writing happens when the author sits down and opens a vein. With vulnerability and honesty that is never self-indulgent and always helpful, Patrick inspires, encourages and points us to a better today rather than just vague hope for better days. Vital stuff. Buy it.'
Jeff Lucas, author, speaker, broadcaster

'Patrick's fervour in combating the stigma associated with mental health problems and his passion for providing encouragement and practical support for those who are going through difficult times are evident throughout this book. His approach is to bring together his personal experiences, relevant scripture, insights from behavioural science and the testimonies of others. It is a highly effective and engaging one, and this book is packed with wisdom. Patrick successfully makes a topic that is potentially hard to grasp very relatable.'
Dr Chi-Chi Obuaya, consultant psychiatrist

'I love the idea of bouncing forwards rather than bouncing back. It's a really helpful and hopeful image. Patrick is always honest and vulnerable in the way he writes, which is really refreshing. He's the opposite to finger-wagging. This book offers help to us all, as we *all* struggle with our mental health at some point, to see a way forward and live with hope even when we face life's toughest challenges.'
Debra Green OBE, Founder and Director of Redeeming Our Communities

'Patrick has given us a glimpse of reality for many. He has done so with a level of honesty, openness and gentleness that encourages us to face our challenges with the confidence that we're never alone and that nothing is wasted. Inspirational, down-to-earth, real and refreshing.'
Justin Humphreys, CEO (Safeguarding) of Thirtyone:eight

'In *Bouncing Forwards*, Patrick gives us a recipe for personal resilience distilled from his own often painful experience and without any cocktail of spiritual platitudes or counterfeit optimism. A good read for living through a pandemic.'
Lord Richard Chartres

'Resilience is more than just a buzz word – it is a science. It is not a panacea or "cure for everything" but it is about psychologically proven ways to improve our mental health. This is for the sake of ourselves and those around us. In this blend of personal story and research review, Patrick gives us a path worth following. He also brings in faith, one of the domains most proven to build resilience but usually overlooked by secular books on the subject. If you want to fly over life's difficulties – don't read on. If you want to bounce forwards and live through the bumps that will inevitably come our way, then this is a helpful guide.'
Dr Rob Waller, consultant psychiatrist and Co-Director of mindandsoulfoundation.org

'I love reading and I read a lot of books. I think I could be considered a binge reader as I usually get through a book fairly quickly as I always like to get to the end. That's what I expected to do with *Bouncing Forwards*. I had it on my to read list and knew I would enjoy it; Patrick is a compelling and honest speaker and author and I knew I would eat it up, but something happened that I didn't expect with this book. I couldn't just whip through it. It wasn't that it wasn't compelling or that I didn't want to get to the next part, I did, it was more that God used it to open up things within me that I had pressed down and he wanted me to deal with. I believe we all have those things within us. Wounds that we just assume we have to accept and move on from, some wounds that only we know about that still impact today. Through reading this book I was compelled, no, moved, to spend time facing things that God only knows and pouring them out, bringing them to God and being more honest with myself than I have been in a while. It was a cleansing experience and one that I intend to continue beyond reading this book. Patrick is disarmingly honest in his writing and manages to combine biblical wisdom and secular knowledge in a way that is both understandable and real. The real-life stories told show vulnerability as well as hope, not that things always turn out as people want or expect but that God is with us in whatever we go through and cares more than we could ever imagine.

If you think you have it all together, great, read this book and you will get an understanding about how God helps those who are struggling, and this will give you empathy and broader knowledge about other people's pain. If like so many of us you are living with wounds, grief, anxiety, self-esteem issues, trauma or just putting on a front, you will find this book refreshingly honest, incredibly helpful and very practical.'
Paula Stringer, UK CEO of Christians Against Poverty

'We've known Patrick for many years and have always loved the way he carries great hope and a depth of honesty. He has a unique way of inspiring and comforting people. We've no doubt that this fantastic and incredibly timely book will offer much peace and support to the many of us who are trying to navigate the chaos and uncertainty of life.'
Tim and Rachel Hughes, Gas Street, Birmingham

'Such an important book on such an important subject! This books hums with the kind of profundity and spiritual power that only comes from personal experience and deep reflection.'
Paul Harcourt, National Leader, New Wine England

'This wonderful book is so incredibly honest, insightful, biblical and practical. It will be a great help to many as we all seek to flourish in the face of the challenges in front of us. I thank the Lord that Patrick has written it as it's such a vital book for our day.'
Gavin Calver, General Director of Evangelical Alliance

'This book is an incredible gift for the cultural moment we find ourselves in. Patrick's own testimony after experiencing deep loss, doubt and pain, is that by God's grace, he didn't just bounce back, he bounced forwards with a renewed sense of faith, calling and hope for the future. This book is therefore written by a guide who has walked the path of adversity, knows the terrain, and lovingly offers wisdom, direction and courage for fellow travellers. For anyone losing hope in their ability to bounce back after a season of struggle, this book will birth faith that you can more than just bounce back, you can bounce forwards into a whole new season.'
Pete Hughes, Senior Pastor of Kings Cross Church, London and author of *All Things New*

'In *Bouncing Forwards*, Patrick has drawn from his many years of working with people whose lives have been broken and shattered by the events of life. He has also drawn from his own challenging experiences. He has turned this breadth of life experience into helping and encouraging others, and demonstrates that it is possible, from a place of brokenness, to be restored. Thank you Patrick.'
Les Isaac, CEO of Ascension Trust and Street Pastors

'Everything Patrick does is infused with authentic, deep truth that resonates in the truest part of our hearts and minds. This book makes me truly thankful to be in the company of people who know the truth that sets us free.'
Danielle Strickland, Kingdom entrepreneur

'This book is a compelling read as Patrick lives out his conviction that vulnerability and authenticity are the best ways to walk through the pain of life. It means he provides empathy, safety and hope through each chapter which bit by bit helps the reader become stronger and more resilient to the inner battles we all face. The mix of wisdom, practical insights and powerful stories make this a book not just to read but to treasure.'
Ness Wilson, Leader of Pioneer UK, Team Leader of Open Heaven Church

'I appreciate Patrick's willingness to be vulnerable in order to help others feel safe about their own struggles. It is vital that we don't just admit it's okay to not be okay, but also have tools to go forward in health and wholeness. In a time of uncertainty its helpful to hear from honest leaders who convey the importance of acknowledging where we come from, the difficulties so many have and are walking through, and one of the best ways for these honest conversations to take place is when leaders are willing to create safe spaces by sharing their own vulnerabilities. I appreciate Patrick's willingness to share not only his own story but the stories of others whom many will relate too. I believe this will help many find encouragement and helpful insights which often leads to personal freedom.'
Christy Wimber, Author and Speaker

BOUNCING FORWARDS

NOTES ON RESILIENCE, COURAGE AND CHANGE

PATRICK REGAN

WITH LIZA HOEKSMA

WAVERLEY ABBEY
RESOURCES

DEDICATION

To my Uncle Barry. I am so sorry life has been so tough for you. I hope you know that what you and Nan sowed into me at a young age has enabled me to do what I do.

Copyright © Patrick Regan, 2021

Published 2021 by Waverley Abbey Resources, an operating name of CWR, Waverley Abbey House, Waverley Lane, Farnham, Surrey GU9 8EP, UK. Registered Charity No. 294387. Registered limited company No. 1990308. Reprinted in 2021, 2022.

The right of Patrick Regan to be identified as the author of this work has been asserted by him in accordance with the Copyright, Designs and Patents Act 1988, sections 77 and 78.

For a list of National Distributors, visit waverleyabbeyresources.org/distributors

Unless otherwise indicated, all Scripture references are from the Holy Bible, New International Version® Anglicised, NIV® Copyright © 1979, 1984, 2011 by Biblica, Inc.® Used by permission. All rights reserved worldwide. Scripture quotations marked NRSV are from the New Revised Standard Version Bible, copyright © 1989 the Division of Christian Education of the National Council of the Churches of Christ in the United States of America. Used by permission. All rights reserved. Scripture quotations marked The Message are taken from THE MESSAGE, copyright © 1993, 2002, 2018 by Eugene H. Peterson. Used by permission of NavPress. All rights reserved. Represented by Tyndale House Publishers, Inc.

Every effort has been made to ensure that this book contains the correct permissions and references, but if anything has been inadvertently overlooked, the Publisher will be pleased to make the necessary arrangements at the first opportunity. Please contact the Publisher directly.

Concept development and editing by Waverley Abbey Resources.

Design and production by Yeomans and Waverley Abbey Resources.

Printed in the UK by Page Bros.

ISBN: 978-1-78951-363-9

ACKNOWLEDGMENTS

Thanks to my special family: Diane, Keziah, Daniel, Abigail and Caleb. I'm so grateful we get to do life together as a team.

I am forever indebted to Liza who is simply a beautiful person and so talented. We have now journeyed through six books together and I could not have done any of this without you.

Special thanks to Ellen, Steven and Liz; I feel privileged that you have allowed us to tell your stories in here. Thanks to Lynette and Mick Brooks for your friendship and your belief in me and Diane. To my very special Kintsugi family, it's such an honour to be your boss and friend. Ludivine Kadimba, we are so proud of you. Jess and Matt Cooper, thanks for your support and your amazing creativity. Joel Harris, you're always such a source of encouragement; I love travelling with you. Alex Newson and Lauren Rusbridge, you guys are the dream team. Mike Coates, thanks so much for the thousands of miles we have travelled together. You often stay in the background and allow me to do what I do; I am so grateful. Jane Diggines and Louise Bethge, I'm so pleased you are part of us now. Thanks to the Kintsugi Hope trustees, especially Simon Barrington; Diane and I feel so blessed to have you as our chair. Erin Docherty, Sarah Pearmain, Adam Temple, Judith Lace, Joby Easow, Audrey Skervin and Elizabeth Neep, thanks for all your support and advice. Jean Allchorne, Jo Topley and Tony Britten, for always cheering us on, and thanks Tony for sharing your story in this book. To all the Kintsugi Hope Wellbeing Group leaders around the UK, too many to mention. Eddie Donaldson, for all your support, especially for allowing me to come to the White House when I desperately needed to crack on; MJ left a great legacy. Tara Cutland Green, without your support the content of this book would not have taken shape in me. Jane Smith, your poems and humility constantly inspire us.

Simon Ray, thank you for designing the cover. Jo Stockdale, thank you for your amazing editing. Thank you also to everyone at Waverley Abbey Resources who has worked on the book: Janette Godfrey, Yasmin Bennett, Jonny Byczok, Michele LeTissier, Joy McIlroy, Mark Markiewicz and Anthony Wilkins.

A huge thank you to all my friends who so kindly endorsed this book, taking time out of their busy schedules to read it – especially Amy Orr-Ewing for writing the foreword.

Last but by no means least, my wider family for all their love and support: Mum, Dad, Becky, John, David, Esther and the Whicker clan.

CONTENTS

FOREWORD
BY DR AMY ORR-EWING

'Now let me at the truth that will refresh my broken mind.'
Mumford & Sons, *The Cave*

In Bouncing Forwards, Patrick Regan takes us on a journey beyond acknowledging our pain, trauma and anxiety when life hurts – as important as those things are – into the terrain of how we might embrace resilience and healing. Some of us will be picking up this book feeling a need for truth that might refresh our broken minds. If that resonates, keep reading – this is a book for you!

I first met Patrick when our two families lived in Peckham, London. He was the inspirational founder and Director of XLP, an organisation working to serve young people in the city, and my husband and I were leading at All Saints Church Peckham. Patrick's vision, passion, energy and devotion to the cause God had called him to shone through his life. He radiated Jesus' love and compassion. He and Diane are the real deal. Over the years, jobs and circumstances have changed, but I have continually been encouraged by their work and ministry. As Patrick has opened up about his own health challenges in recent years, including mental health, the truth is that he has struck a nerve with many. I believe that every single one of us will face the challenges that mental health issues bring, whether personally or as we support loved ones.

This means Patrick's message in this new book is both timely and helpful.

I've been listening to Patrick over these last few years – as he has spoken honestly and openly about suffering and doubt in *When Faith Gets Shaken*. I've noticed how powerfully the Lord has moved through the truth, vulnerability, honesty and courage of the messenger. I've been on a journey myself, too, of experiencing the aftermath of devastating trauma and processing how our loving God gently carries us through valleys of tears. How desperately we the Church in this generation need to hear and know the truth that God is big enough for our questions and our pain. That he welcomes us as we actually are – including in the midst of trauma, devastation or depression. That he is not interested in us pretending to be compliant, religious do-gooders. Far from it. The Bible gives powerful voice to human responses to pain that express doubt, anger and confusion that terrible things are happening. The psalmist asks: 'My God, my God, why have you forsaken me? Why are you so far from saving me, so far from my cries of anguish?' (Psa. 22:1–2). The book of Job tells the story of a man who later in life was commended as a 'righteous man' but who experiences terrible suffering. At one point he says to God: 'Does it please you to oppress me, to spurn the work of your hands, while you smile on the plans of the wicked?' (Job 10:3). The prophet Habakkuk asks how long he is expected to continue shouting out to God that there is violence, pain and injustice while God appears to do nothing at all about it: 'How long, LORD, must I call for help, but you do not listen? Or cry out to you, "Violence!" but you do not save?' (Hab. 1:2). The very same questions and frustrations that we experience in the midst of our suffering today were articulated by people in pain whose words ended up in the Bible. God wanted us to know that it is OK to feel as we do when we suffer – and to express our anger and frustration to him, so when we feel 'How much longer are you going to let this go on?', 'Why are you so distant?', 'Why aren't you answering or helping?' we are not alone. Patrick has lived and taught the reality that when life is hard it is OK not to be OK. I really admire his honesty and courage. I have found his vulnerability to be a real strength in his writing and leadership.

And now Patrick has written this raw and yet approachable new book, *Bouncing Forwards*. In the following pages, Patrick explores what it really looks like to live as a Christian with pain, suffering, trauma, anxiety and grief. With a deep conviction that every single person is unimaginably loved and special, made in the image of a loving God, *Bouncing Forwards* takes us on a journey through resilience, relationships, grief and pain. Patrick skilfully blends stories, quotations and hard-won personal insights to help us imagine how we might go back to move forwards, and see that nothing in our experience of life, however negative, need be wasted. In a similar vein, the poet Mary Oliver put it like this: 'Someone I loved once gave me a box full of darkness. It took me years to understand that this, too, was a gift.'

Patrick then asks us to consider what success really means in life, and to begin to shape our priorities and decisions accordingly, and he reminds us of the power of kindness and gratitude.

In the finale – Go Gently – Patrick himself says, 'I want to bounce forwards, demonstrating emotional agility when my feelings are threatening to overwhelm me. As Jesus walked alongside his friends on the Emmaus road, I long to walk with friends in their pain.'

In this book this is exactly what he does. Thank you, dear friend!

Dr Amy Orr-Ewing
Oxford, 2020

INTRODUCTION
A STRANGE BACKDROP

At the start of 2020, I was working on an idea for a book on resilience and how we recover from painful things that happen in our lives. I was intrigued by the idea of how we can thrive, not just when we've come through adversity, but right there in the midst of it. My previous book, *Honesty Over Silence*, had a clear message that it's OK not to be OK. It was a cry for more authenticity, integrity and humility when looking at our mental and emotional health, seeking to break the shackles of shame many of us struggle with when we're not doing so well. Though it felt vulnerable to write, it turned out to be what many people needed to hear. Readers responded with such relief that someone was talking about how hard things can be, letting them know they aren't strange or abnormal; life can just be difficult sometimes.

With this new book I wanted to continue the journey. I didn't want people to get stuck in not being OK; I wanted to look at how we can flourish, even if our challenging circumstances don't change. I came up with a working title of *How to Be OK When Life Isn't*, wrote a proposal and sent it to my publisher. We were still touring with *Honesty Over Silence*, so life was very busy, and the new book went on the back burner. Then, on 22 March, I wrote this in my journal:

The world has changed. It feels like we are living in a horror film due to coronavirus. No one except key workers are allowed to travel to work, no one can go to pubs, gyms, schools or churches. There are no gatherings and everyone has to keep two metres apart. Mum and Dad are no longer allowed to see the kids or give them a hug. It's heartbreaking and so hard to get your head round. Life is so fragile. My anxiety has gone sky high worrying about catching the virus or my family getting it. Diane is super stressed at the prospect of all four kids being home all the time, all with very different needs, while we're trying to work at the same time. I am so scared and so tired but still I'm hoping that, somehow, through this, we will get closer to God.

It was overwhelming for everyone. I was especially worried about my sister and mum, who are both nurses, and my 17-year-old daughter, who started work as a domestic assistant in a care home. My wife, Diane, and I needed to move all our charity's work around mental health online at a time when people's mental health was plummeting and demand for support was greater than ever. The world changed for everyone in what felt like the blink of an eye, and we were all coping with new pressures and strains, ranging from the huge burden of the loss of loved ones through to the uncertainties of seeing empty supermarket shelves.

The country was still reeling and in the throes of this pandemic when many woke up to the fact there was another pandemic that had been at work for centuries: racism. On 25 May, a 46-year-old black man called George Floyd was killed in Minneapolis during an arrest for allegedly using a counterfeit banknote. A white police officer knelt on George's neck for almost nine minutes while he was handcuffed and lying face down. He begged for his life, repeatedly saying, 'I can't breathe'. A second and third officer further restrained him, while a fourth stopped bystanders from intervening. The shocking video, filmed by a passer-by, went viral and was seen across the world, triggering demonstrations and protests in over 2,000 US cities and around the world against continued police brutality and racism. George Floyd's last words, 'I can't breathe', resonated with the experience of many people of colour who have been suffocated for far too long by white supremacy.

Like so many, I was horrified at the injustice of racism that continues to be perpetrated today. Against this backdrop, was now the time for me to write anything? Diane encouraged me that resilience was exactly what people needed to hear about. In the midst of a global health pandemic and with the backdrop of unrest over endemic racism, we need the principles of resilience more than ever. This would really put my research to the test. The world had never seemed less OK to me; was there really a way to thrive regardless?

BOUNCING BACK

Resilience is often talked about as 'bouncing back', in the way that an elastic band is stretched and then goes back into shape. Chris Johnstone, in his book *Seven Ways to Build Resilience*, explores this further by talking about the difference between a tennis ball and a tomato. If you squeeze a tennis ball, it bends back into shape. If you throw it against the ground, it bounces back. In contrast, do the same to a tomato and all you get is a mess. Johnstone points out that this is only one view of resilience. What happens if you bury a tomato and a tennis ball in soil? After a number of years, the ball will likely have started to decompose and be useless. On the other hand, given the right circumstances, the seeds in the tomato may have taken root and given birth to new life. You could find new vines ripe with fresh, juicy tomatoes. Johnstone says, 'When adversity is followed by new growth, where we rise again but in a different form, we can think of this as bouncing forward.'[1]

As I reflected on all that had happened in recent months, I realised I didn't want to 'bounce back'. We've been through a crisis, and when I look back I want to be able to see that, although it's been incredibly challenging, it has changed me for the better. That's my hope for us as a society too, that out of these terrible times we'll see positive change as well. It's clear that the horrific murder of George Floyd woke the world up to changes that need to be made to bring equality. COVID-19 has already brought many terrible changes, but we also quickly saw some positives. People who we previously described as 'low-skilled workers' were suddenly our 'key workers' as we realised we couldn't live without them. Many workers who previously spent hours a day commuting and weren't able to see their families were suddenly at home. Neighbours checked up on each other more than ever before, forming online groups to support one another and provide practical help. We all began to realise how much we appreciated friends and family who we could no longer see, many putting in extra phone calls and Zooms to stay in touch far better than they had previously. There's a possibility that this crisis will make many of us re-evaluate what's important and prompt us to live differently in the future.

That's not to say that resilience is just looking at the positives, pretending the bad stuff isn't there or doesn't impact us. Quite the opposite. In this book we will look at why pretending everything is OK when it isn't can be so harmful, and how we can face up to the difficult circumstances we're in without losing hope. We'll explore the difference between acceptance and resignation, how we move through grief and trauma, the nature and benefits of being emotionally agile, and having a growth mindset – finding meaning in hard times and learning about how we grow in those seasons.

In this book I talk about my Christian faith as it is very important to me. I hope that you'll still find what I have to say accessible even if you don't share that same faith. Let me reassure you at the outset, faith for me isn't about black and white answers or telling others what to do or think.

I hope that whoever you are, whatever your background, whatever challenges the present day is throwing at you, you'll get something out of this book and it will encourage you and bring you hope. The principles of resilience, courage and change are invaluable to us all.

To my relief, all the research I've done agrees that resilience isn't simply about being tougher and trying harder; this isn't a book that will tell you to get your head down and get on with it. Resilience also isn't a fixed trait, it's something we can grow and develop in.

If you've read any of my books before, you'll know I don't come at any of these topics as an expert but as a pilgrim who is on the same journey as you. I have drawn on so many sources, authors, stories and research to learn all I can about resilience. I look to the Bible and theology teachers as well as to many of the finest minds in psychology, life coaching, activitism and business studies. As I've read, researched and listened, I've become even more wedded to this idea that resilience is key. As one author put it, 'More than education, more than experience, more than training, a person's level of resilience will determine who succeeds and who fails. That's true in the cancer ward, it's true in the Olympics, and it's true in the boardroom.'[2]

I am always in awe of people who persevere during hard times and manage to keep going, growing in their relationship with God and staying kind and open, loving and caring, despite what they've been through, often creating something positive from their own pain. I've tried to tell some of the stories of people who have inspired me here, including Ellen, who lost her baby halfway through her pregnancy; Steven, who has dealt with many traumas and has still gone on to be a compassionate man who looks out for others in his community; and Liz, who has suffered from a debilitating lung condition her entire life. If you've read my previous books, *When Faith Gets Shaken* and *Honesty Over Silence*, you'll know I love to give other people the opportunity to tell their stories. I think it's really important to look at topics like resilience, courage and change from different perspectives, genders and ethnicities. The story chapters in this book are authentic and earth what we are discussing in real life experience.

To accept our circumstances takes courage and vulnerability. I hope that as we journey through this book together we can explore these topics with openness, honesty and vulnerability. It may be hard at times but I am sure it will be worth it. K.J. Ramsey, in her lovely book *This Too Shall Last*, writes about how joy and sorrow coexist. She comments, 'Jesus says, "Come to me, all of you are weary and burdened and I will give you rest." Jesus acknowledges your burden. He doesn't shame it, doesn't label it and doesn't proclaim it to be a barrier to being a faithful Christian. With outstretched hand he invites you to rest. But first you must acknowledge what he already sees with his open, kind eyes. To receive the rest Jesus offers, you must acknowledge your weariness and your burden.'[3]

CHAPTER 1

ACCEPTANCE NOT DEFEAT

A few years ago, two spiritual giants met to discuss one of life's biggest questions: how do we find joy in the face of life's inevitable suffering? These were two men who knew about suffering. Not in a theoretical sense, not second-hand from hearing other people's stories, but as part of their own lived experience. Archbishop Desmond Tutu and the 14th Dalai Lama have both known many years of oppression and exile, and yet they met to talk about the subject of joy.

Their conversations went on to be the basis of *The Book of Joy: Lasting Happiness in a Changing World*. The book talks about coming to a place where we have 'the ability to accept our life in all its pain, imperfection and beauty', saying, 'Acceptance, it must be pointed out, is the opposite to resignation... Acceptance... allows us to engage with life on its own terms rather than rail against the fact that life is not as we would wish... So many of the causes of suffering come from our reacting to the people, places, things and circumstances in our lives, rather than accepting them.'[1]

If these words had come from someone else, they might not have had such an impact on me. But these two are poverty fighters, activists, people who have won the Nobel Peace Prize for the work they've done. They're not the types to sit back passively, so it hit me that acceptance of your circumstances and resignation about them are very different things.

If you've heard me speak or have read one of my previous books, you'll know the theme of suffering is something I've grown increasingly interested in. I've experienced for myself, and seen all around me, the pain that life can bring. I know all too well that you can be ticking along OK only to suddenly find yourself on your knees in physical, mental, emotional and spiritual anguish.

As I look back at some difficult years for me personally, I can see I've spent much of the time waiting for my circumstances to get better. When I was diagnosed with a degenerative knee condition and told I needed two lots of major surgery that would take years to recover from, I just wanted it done. I wanted that season over so I could get back to normal life. When my dad got cancer, I wanted the treatment to be finished and for him to be well. When it looked like the charity I ran might run out of money, I wanted a big donation to come in so I didn't have to worry anymore. And then there were the situations that would have no return to life before them: my wife Diane having a miscarriage, my daughter Abigail being diagnosed with additional needs; the loss of another young person in our community that my charity had been working hard to keep away from gang violence. My coping strategy of wishing myself into the future would make no difference there. Should I be praying for miracles or did I need to find another way to live?

I had tried to keep going, to keep battling through, but I felt like I had spent years running on near empty. I would get within metres of an emotional cliff edge, realise how close I was and then retreat a couple of steps. Safer but not safe. I was aware enough to realise this probably wasn't an ideal way to be living but I couldn't see any alternative. There was so much need, so many things I wanted to do, so many people I wanted to help, so much going on at home. The teaching I was hearing made me think I needed to pray harder, seek God more, put in more hours reading my Bible, fight the enemy, not allow negative thinking to take root in my life... The list was exhaustive and exhausting. I would hear stories of how heroes of the faith would get up at 4am and spend hours seeking God, so I would resolve to make that my daily practice. (Then I would get to bed at midnight and realise there was no way that was going to happen.)

I was trying to please everyone and not managing to please anyone, least of all myself. My worries about my health grew but I didn't tell anyone. Part of my coping strategy for dealing with adversity was to keep quiet and keep pushing though. Unsurprisingly, my mental health started to go downhill. The pains in my chest and arms were now very regular and I was struggling to cope. Ironically, to the outside world my life looked great: I was going through a phase of being constantly asked to speak on TV and at large events, my charity was being visited by members of the Royal Family. From that respect, life couldn't have been better. But behind the scenes I was a wreck. As my anxiety shot up, so did my guilt; surely I wasn't trusting God enough? I felt like a total failure and thought God must be pretty fed up with me.

One day I came home from work and said to Diane, 'I can't do this anymore. I've got pains in my chest. I need to get to A&E.' At the hospital I had an ECG to check my heart and a whole bunch of other tests, then I waited for hours for the results, wondering how serious it was and convincing myself of all sorts of awful scenarios. 'Let's wait and see,' Diane said, trying to reassure me. Eventually we sat down with a doctor who said they couldn't find anything physically wrong with me. 'Do you have a stressful job?' she asked. And there it was. That was the moment I finally faced up to it: physically my body was fine but mentally I was very unwell. My coping mechanisms were not up to the job. Sitting there in A&E, I had to accept that I had real challenges going on and I needed to face up to them and make some changes before it was too late. Of course, Diane had been telling me for years I was going to tumble off the cliff edge one day and I needed to make some drastic changes, but it wasn't until that moment that the penny really dropped for me.

I was given a sabbatical from work. I know some people were thinking it must have been lovely to be given some time off, but the reality was that it was one of the hardest seasons of my life. Everything felt like it was tumbling around me. I felt like such a mess and as though Diane had to pick me up off the floor each day just for me to put one foot in front of the other.

Just as when I was told about my knee condition and had to learn a huge amount of medical language, now I had to learn the language of mental health: anxiety, depression, perfectionism and shame. I needed to accept where I was before I could even think about moving forwards.

Accepting the situation we are in sometimes seems counterintuitive; when our circumstances are hard it's natural to want to fight against them. That makes sense when those circumstances are within our control; taking action can bring about positive change. But what about the things we can't change? Imagine you see someone standing in the middle of some quicksand. Your immediate reaction is to tell them to get out, to move as quickly as they can to safety. If you're the one stuck in quicksand, no doubt your natural reaction is to try your hardest to get out too. The challenge with quicksand is that the more you struggle, the more you sink. The more you fight, the more the quicksand consumes you. Crazy as it seems, the way to get free is to stop struggling and to try to lie as calmly and as flat as you can. This spreads your body weight out and allows you to roll yourself away to safety.

A NEW KIND OF FRIDGE MAGNET

When we're going through a hard time, one of the most common verses we turn to is Jeremiah 29:11, which says:

> 'For I know the plans I have for you,' declares the Lord, 'plans to prosper you and not to harm you, plans to give you hope and a future.'

There are probably more fridge magnets, posters, postcards and T-shirts with this verse on than any other verse in the Bible. It's a great 'one-size-fits-all' encouragement. It's reassuring to believe that God has plans for us, especially when the world feels chaotic and out of our control. Who doesn't want to think that God wants good things for them, especially when they're facing challenging circumstances and finding life hard? We read it, we breath more easily; it's OK, God is going to change things.

Unfortunately, we've taken this verse completely out of context and so we've missed out on what God was really saying. Far from ruining the party and stealing your hope, I want to offer you something deeper than a simple reading of this verse allows.

The book of Jeremiah was written during the time when the Babylonian army had invaded and destroyed Jerusalem and the people of God had been taken into exile by King Nebuchadnezzar. Tens of thousands of Hebrews were marched across several hundred miles of desert to live in a place where Yahweh was not known. There was no temple of God to visit, they could make no Levitical sacrifices, and it put an end to their calendar of festivals and celebrations that marked their relationship with God and their place as his chosen people. They had to live by a wholly different set of values. Put simply, they were aliens in a foreign land. The whole book of Lamentations is devoted to expressing their crushing sadness; they were a people who felt abandoned, rootless, vulnerable and orphaned.

Have you ever experienced that? I'm guessing, as you've picked up a book on resilience, you've known some hard times and are maybe even experiencing one now. I wonder if you've ever felt abandoned by God. Rootless and untethered from all you've known and believed to be true. Confused about the direction your life has taken. Vulnerable in your pain. Have you ever asked God, 'What's going on here?' Have you ever felt like you just don't understand? Like you can hang on to your belief in God – even if only by your fingertips – but you just have no idea what is happening? That's where the Israelites were at. So when a prophet called Hananiah declared that God was saying he would restore Israel within two years and bring back the temple treasures that Nebuchadazzar had taken to Babylon (Jer. 28) you can imagine how they rejoiced. It was all going to be OK! These were the words they'd longed to hear.

The prophet Jeremiah would have been happy to see it fulfilled too, only he knew it wasn't a word from God. It was against this backdrop that Jeremiah wrote a letter from Jerusalem to the elders, priests, prophets and all the people who had been exiled. In it he told them what

God had actually said: that it would be 70 years before God would bring them out of that place (29:10). This is what God had to say:

> 'Build houses and settle down; plant gardens and eat what they produce. Marry and have sons and daughters; find wives for your sons and give your daughters in marriage, so that they too may have sons and daughters. Increase in number there; do not decrease. Also, seek the peace and prosperity of the city to which I have carried you into exile. Pray to the Lord for it, because if it prospers, you too will prosper.' Yes, this is what the Lord Almighty, the God of Israel, says: 'Do not let the prophets and diviners among you deceive you. Do not listen to the dreams you encourage them to have. They are prophesying lies to you in my name. I have not sent them,' declares the Lord. (Jer. 29:5–9)

If God's people were going to be in exile for two years, they could wait it out. It would be slow and painful but they would get there. What God was actually saying was that they were going to be there for 70 years. Seventy! Imagine the worst moment of your pain and then being told the situation wouldn't shift for 70 years. The people so desperately longed to go home that Hananiah's promise of two years was far more appealing.

God wasn't trying to depress them. He wanted to make sure they didn't waste 70 years. He told them not to expect things to change quickly but to make the best of the circumstances there were in. He told them to plant gardens and grow their own food because they would be around to enjoy its fruit. He told them not to put their life on hold waiting for when they were free but to marry and have children there. This wasn't a time to hunker down and lick their wounds. He didn't want them to be inward looking, gritting their teeth to get through. God wanted his people to be generous and kind; he wanted them to reach out and help others. In short, he told them to *live*. He was saying, 'Don't wait until you leave Babylon. Live *now*. Make the most of where you are and what you have, even though it's not what you would have chosen, even though you feel abandoned and alone. Don't miss out on what I want to do in these hard circumstances waiting for an easier day to come.'

I don't know about you, but wow, those words hit home to me. How often do we make the mistake of not living in the moment? We wait for the healing, the answer to the prayer, the fulfilment of our dreams, and miss so much of what God is doing here and now. We refuse to plant a garden where we are, longing for a better garden in the future, and in doing so we miss out on the fruit we could have enjoyed. We long for the Promised Land and we forget that God is at work even in the desert.

What might life look like if instead of waiting, we learnt the art of resilience and could thrive in the midst of adversity right now? What if we made the most of the place where we found ourselves in, even if – or perhaps especially when – circumstances aren't ideal?

The brilliant Liz Carter (who tells her story later in this book) writes, 'Jeremiah didn't give false hope by promising that this future would be theirs for the taking right now in their lives, instead he advised them to comply with and participate in this situation. God was extending hope to those in a horrendous situation, but not making a promise that life would suddenly become free of difficulty.'[2]

NO END IN SIGHT?

Most of us feel like we can endure anything when we know it's going to come to an end, but what about when we don't know when or even if it might change?

Admiral James Stockdale was in a POW camp in Vietnam in the 1960s. He faced being pulled away from his labour at any point and tortured, and he didn't know if he would ever be released or see his loved ones again. Despite the horrific circumstances, he was convinced that no matter what happened he could turn this experience into a defining moment in his life that he wouldn't want to trade for anything else. Eventually he made it out, and when asked years later, 'Who didn't make it out like you?' he quickly replied that it was the optimists, the ones who said, 'We'll be out by Christmas.' Christmas would come and go and they'd say, 'We'll definitely be home by next Christmas.' But that too would come and go with no change. It sounds like they had the right attitude: think positive, keep your hopes up and everything will be OK. This is often the pseudo spiritual advice perpetrated by our society, but in actual fact, this wishful thinking did them no good.

Instead it crushed their spirits and broke their hearts. Maybe this is what Proverbs 13:12 means when it says that 'hope deferred makes the heart sick'.

Jim Collins, author of *Good to Great*, calls the attitude of Admiral Stockdale the Stockdale Paradox, and says, 'We need on the one-hand unwavering faith that you can and will prevail in the end and, at the same time, you need the discipline to confront the brutal facts as they actually are.'[3] Collins says he saw that leaders of great companies embodied the same duality. They led their companies through years of difficulty with faith they would get to the other side, and at the same time could confront the reality of where they were at that moment.

Facing up to the facts isn't about despairing and saying, 'I give up. Life is always going to be hard.' It's about acknowledging the reality of your circumstances and accepting them, saying that even if the longed-for day comes, when things are different, this is still your reality today.

RESISTANCE VS RESILIENCE

One of things that has really helped me is Acceptance and Commitment Therapy (ACT). When we're feeling pain, fear, confusion and other negative emotions, our instinct is to try to run away from them. We see them as intruders, there to ruin our lives, and we want to get as far away as possible. We avoid them, we run from them and we try to deny their very presence. No wonder we wind up exhausted. ACT suggests that we can engage with our emotions in a different way. By accepting that our emotions are the reasonable response to situations that have been painful, we can begin to see that they don't need to stop us moving forwards.[4]

It's a bit like having an unwanted guest at a party. One that keeps showing up again and again no matter how many times you show them the door. One choice is to guard the door all night, missing out on the party to try to keep them out, and when they return to seethe quietly about their presence. This doesn't mean they go away, but it is likely to ruin your evening. An alternative is to accept their presence and to get on with the party anyway. You don't ignore them – it's quite hard to ignore a rude guest – but you talk to your friends and start having an OK time. Then you realise that when you're not trying to kick them out, they've actually got some redeeming qualities. Maybe they're hard to see underneath all the things that drive you mad, but actually they're not as bad as you thought they were. They might even become someone you invite to your next party.[5]

We think that fighting our negative emotions is the best way to protect ourselves, but actually we can wind up exhausted because we can't get rid of them. Accepting them sounds negative: doesn't that mean giving up and giving in? No! It's about getting curious about them. We can't control them. We can't avoid them. But we can come to a place of accepting that they're there. As one author put it: 'ACT encourages us towards more helpful ways of thinking which means we don't just feel more able to tackle the challenges we have, but to live the life we are meant to while we do that.'[6]

The opposite of acceptance and commitment is control and avoidance. I don't think I'm alone in struggling with the feeling of being out of control, but that is our reality. We can only control a tiny proportion of life and we need to find a way to be OK with that. We can fight it as much as we want but it's not going to get us more control.

BOUNCING FORWARDS

As I mentioned in the Introduction, sometimes resilience is described as the ability to bounce back from difficulties or crises, but many have started to acknowledge that when we've been through significant pain or trauma, it alters us for good. For some of us it's a physical change: we suffer the loss of a limb or live with a degenerative condition that has a considerable impact on our day-to-day life and our ability to enjoy the things we once did. Some of us lose someone we love, and their presence leaves a huge gap in our life that no one else can fill. Often there's a change in our hearts: we now know something of how painful life can be in a way we'd never experienced before. Our eyes have been opened and we lose something of our innocence. My point isn't that suffering only causes negative change – we'll look at the good that can come out of it throughout this book. What I'm trying to say is that we can't ignore it. We can't pretend these things haven't had an impact on us and expect ourselves to be the same person we were before. That will leave us constantly striving for the impossible.

In expecting ourselves to go back to how we were before, we're setting ourselves up for failure. We're comparing our current self with one who has been through much less. Life leaves its scars, and I've always found it thought-provoking that even in his resurrection body, Jesus still held the scars of earth (John 20:20,27).

A more helpful way to look at it is that rather than bouncing back, we bounce forwards. Recent research suggests that resilience isn't going back to our pre-trauma/loss selves, it's moving forwards to a new way of being.

In some strange ways, I didn't want to bounce back; I didn't want to lose the lessons I'd learned, and I knew I was changed. Pain can be a gift; it can highlight that there's an issue to stop us from continuing damaging behaviour. Bouncing forwards means we don't stay in a constant state of crisis but we go on day by day, changed, and hopefully more accepting. We can't wipe the pain from our lives, so we have a choice: try to ignore it and allow it to break us, or work with it and see if it can lead us somewhere new.

CHAPTER 2

RESILIENCE AND RELATIONSHIPS

When I think about some of my heroes, they are men and women who have persisted despite many setbacks and obstacles. Some are well known, like Martin Luther King, Desmond Tutu and Mother Teresa, others are people I've had the privilege of walking alongside in life and seeing how they've kept going despite the odds.

One common thread running through the lives of all the resilient people I can think of is that they didn't achieve anything on their own. I was fortunate enough to meet Desmond Tutu when he came to visit the urban youth work charity I set up, XLP, and one of the things he said to me was, 'If you ever achieve anything, it's always on the shoulders of others.' Resilient people are not lone rangers. We all need people who will journey with us through the joy and heartache of life. After a survey about wellbeing in the workplace, the authors Tom Rath and Jim Harter said, 'We discovered that the single best predictor is not what people are doing – but who they are doing it with.'[1]

Harvard psychiatrist George Vaillant, reporting a study that followed a group of men over a 70-year period, summed up the results by identifying the most powerful factor influencing life satisfaction 'as warmth of relationships throughout life'.[2]

My favourite poet is Maya Angelou, and I find reading about her life as fascinating as reading her poems. Her childhood was unpredictable and included many moves and many homes. She also suffered a period of devastating violence that left her mute for almost five years. Even after she recovered, her life remained tumultuous. She was devastated by the assassinations of her friends and colleagues Malcolm X and Martin Luther King, and yet, Dr Angelou persisted, as she wrote in what is one of her most famous poems, *Still I Rise*. She knew the racial injustice in the world first hand and saw its horrors, but she refused to quit. Something she said that I have found so helpful is, 'I'm not sure if resilience is ever achieved alone. Experience allows us to learn from example. But if we have someone who loves us – I don't mean who indulges us, but who loves us enough to be on our side – then it's easier to grow resilience, to grow belief in self, to grow self-esteem. And it's self-esteem that allows a person to stand up.'[3]

Going back to that famous verse we talked about from Jeremiah 29, we need to remember that the prophet wasn't writing to an individual but to a whole community of people. The 'you' in 'I have plans to prosper you' is plural, so it means 'you all'. I have plans to prosper *you all*, together. We live in such an individualistic society that we take the verse as a personal promise for us and, while I do believe God has plans for us as individuals, it was written to the people in exile who would succeed not as individuals with individual plans but as part of a community.

In Africa they have the word *unbuntu* which literally means, 'that a person is a person through other people'. It is about sharing our common humanity, our 'oneness'.

The theologians Stanley Grenz and John Franke explain in their book *Beyond Foundationalism* just how a community 'turns the gaze of its members toward the future'. The future in Jeremiah is one that is bright—one that everyone in the community seeks through prayer and worship as their collective future hope. Many of us desperately want to know the plan that God has for us as individuals, but let the prophet Jeremiah remind us that the future isn't all about us, and that it might not look how we think. As one author put it, 'Even more important than our decision about which college to attend, which city to move to or what job offer to take, is the future hope of the Kingdom of God foretold by the prophets and fulfilled in the reign of our now and coming King. In this way, the promise of Jeremiah 29:11 is bigger than any one of us—and far better.'[4]

CRACKED POTS

Sometimes we feel like a less valuable member of the community when we feel broken or are going through hard times. We look to the people we see as having it all together and admire their contribution while belittling our own and wondering if people are fed up with us because we can't offer more. We can feel like we're not enough without ever examining where that feeling comes from or if it's actually true. We think we're not thin enough, clever enough, funny enough or wealthy enough. But who gets to define what enough is? We spend our lives chasing an undefined and therefore impossible goal.

I love the story of the cracked pot. There was a man – a water bearer in India, so the story goes – who had two pots. One was whole and one had a large crack in it. Each day he gathered water from the stream and began the long walk home. The whole pot carried its load from the stream to the master's house, whereas the broken pot lost half its water along the way. After two years of feeling like an utter failure, the broken pot apologised to the man and said he was ashamed of himself. 'Why?' asked the water bearer. 'Because of my flaws,' the pot replied. 'Half of the water leaks away as you walk.' The water bearer asked the broken pot to look again at their route from the stream to the house. 'I want you to notice the beautiful flowers along the path,' he said. 'Did you notice that there were flowers only on your side of your path, but not on the other pot's side? That's because I have always known about your flaw, and I took advantage of it. I planted flower seeds on your side of the path, and every day, while we walk back from the stream, you've watered them. For two years I have been able to pick these beautiful flowers to decorate my master's table. Without you being just the way you are, he would not have had this beauty to grace his house.'[5]

I love the way Paul talks about brokenness in his writing

to the Corinthians too. It's not noted as a negative thing but as a way that God shows his power: 'But we have this treasure in jars of clay to show that this all-surpassing power is from God and not from us' (2 Cor. 4:7).

In New Testament times, when making a clay jar they would use the thinnest material possible so it would crack in the kiln. The cracks allowed the light to diffuse out from within when a lamp was placed inside. In other words, the jars were purposely created to be vulnerable, to let the light out. I find this amazing, that we are also designed to be fragile; our vulnerability and brokenness is by design. Why? So that God's love might shine through us. We are not to boast in our earthly strength but we acknowledge a God who works through our weaknesses.

New Testament theologian Paula Gooder, writes, 'Paul's point in 2 Corinthians is that our cracked, imperfect exteriors (in this instance his in particular) are nothing to be ashamed of – they are vital. A well-glazed pot keeps the light in; only a pot riven with cracks can shine God's light in the world. The cracks let the light out.'[6]

As Christians, we are not called to be perfect. We are called to be who we are, with all our cracks and imperfections, knowing that God's glory will shine through those cracks into the world around us. The gold of God's love will mend our brokenness into something far more beautiful than it was before.

Perhaps we can do more good in our brokenness than when we're pretending we have it all together. Sometimes we need a shift in perspective, to see our brokenness through God's eyes. There is a real beauty to brokenness that can help and nourish others. As Henri Nouwen says so beautifully, 'Nobody escapes being wounded. We are all wounded people, whether physically, emotionally, mentally or spiritually. The main question is not "How can we hide our wounds?" so we don't have to be embarrassed, but "How can we put our woundedness in the service of others?" When our wounds cease to be a source of shame, and become a source of healing, we have become wounded healers.'[7]

This requires vulnerability. We have to be honest with ourselves about who we are and where we're at, as well as being honest with other people. The vulnerability guru, Brené Brown says, 'Owning our stories and loving ourselves through that process is the bravest thing that we will ever do.' Because sometimes we don't want to own our stories. Sometimes the hard things we're going through are the things over which we feel the most shame. A lost job, a divorce, a shattered dream, singleness, childlessness, an overwhelming debt, a child that has lost their way in the world... But as Brené says, 'When we deny our stories, they define us. When we own our stories, we get to write a brave new ending.'[8]

TRUE BELONGING

We can try so hard to hide the bits of ourselves we consider weaker and show people the parts of our personalities and lives we think make us look good. We often want to hide away when we're struggling, fearing rejection if people see the truth. From a young age, most of us try to fit in. We want to look like the other kids at school, we want to sound like them, we want to like the things that they like and hate the things that they hate. We often don't grow out of it. I've tried so many times to fit in at church and often felt like the odd one out. I have had so many questions but have been frightened to voice my opinion in case it offends people. I don't want to rock the boat or have people question if I'm really a Christian. The times I have spoken up and it has gone terribly wrong, my brain has taken as evidence I should never do it again. But when I just try to blend in and be how I think people want me to be, I realise not only am I exhausted by the false nature of living like that, I'm also not giving people the opportunity to accept and even love me for who I am.

To quote Brené Brown again, she says, 'True belonging is the spiritual practice of believing in and belonging to yourself so deeply that you can share your most authentic self with the world... True belonging doesn't require you to change who you are, it requires you to be who you are.'[9]

There is a key distinction between belonging and fitting in: 'Belonging is being accepted for you. Fitting in is being accepted for being like everyone else.'[10]

Fitting in is exhausting. Belonging is life-giving. I want to stop trying to fit in and earn everyone's approval but instead be the real me – aware of my brokenness and flaws but no less deserving of a place at the table, or pew, regardless. To do that, there are some things I need to learn to let go of.

When we started our charity, Kintsugi Hope, we were inspired by the kintsugi artwork where broken pottery is mended with golden glue to become something beautiful. We started wellbeing groups to support people's mental health and emotional wellbeing, and invited friends from our community to join our small group, many of whom have no faith background. Each week I felt like I got to know people better as we talked about the issues that were really affecting our lives, and I began to realise that we are all so similar. One week Diane asked us all to write down our biggest fears on a piece of paper and put it in an envelope. We put our envelope on the table and picked up another one at random, taking turns to read aloud the fears within. There were ten of us there that night and four of us had written 'health anxiety', including me. When it was read out for the fourth time, I joked, 'I'm not the only one then!' I asked, 'Anyone else get a headache, Google it and then think you have a brain tumour?' Everyone laughed; they could relate and I wasn't alone. As writer Mark Manson says, 'The truth is that there is no such thing as a personal problem. If you have a problem the chances are millions of other people have had it in the past, have it now or are going to have it in the future.'[11]

As a group we were so different; we were different ages, from different backgrounds, and with different life experiences, but we all felt safe to be ourselves. Author C.S. Lewis said, 'Friendship is born at that moment when one person says to another: what! You too? I thought I was the only one.'[12] It feels so safe to share how you feel and have others understand, empathise and sit with you in your discomfort and weakness. Far from pushing people away, it draws us closer. The group was special, a safe place where I belonged and didn't feel I had to try to fit in.

Of course, this doesn't mean we must pour our hearts out to everyone in order to be resilient. Most of us can only sustain a small number of deep and genuine friendships where both parties feel truly safe to be our real selves. When we know we're loved, regardless of our weaknesses, it can help us work on the things we want to change. Coming back to Maya Angelou's point, we're not talking about having people who indulge us and say we don't need to work on certain aspects of ourselves, we're talking about having people in our corner who love us regardless of where we are on our journey. I love this quote from Michelle Obama: 'It is not about being perfect. It's not about where you get yourself in the end. There is a power in allowing yourself to be known and heard, in owning your unique story, in using your authentic voice. And there's a grace in being willing to know and hear others. This, for me, is how we become.'[13]

THIS IS ME

If you're a fan of *The Greatest Showman* you'll already be singing to yourself just reading that subtitle. If, like me, a singing circus is not your cup of tea, stay with me. *The Greatest Showman* tells the story of P.T. Barnum, a man who dreams of making money so his family can escape poverty. He stumbles on the idea of putting on a show using unique people; finding people who were considered too tall, too small, too large; people who had amazing abilities but had been outcast by society, like the bearded lady with her stunning singing voice. Barnum takes this bunch of outcasts with low self-esteem and creates a hugely popular show. In the process, he creates a family, with a real sense of belonging, love and acceptance. There's an incredible video you can watch on YouTube that shows the cast rehearsing the anthemic song, *This is Me*. Keala Settle, who played the beaded lady, said she was so nervous and scared singing the song in front of the cast that she stood firmly behind the music stand. The producer tried to encourage her to move towards the middle of the room and really own the message of the song, which is about being comfortable and confident to show your true self to the world. In the video, Keala begins timidly, but as she finds her voice she sings, 'I am not scared to be seen' and walks into the middle of the room. Still looking terrified, she turns around to the backing singers, and then something wonderful happens, she starts to believe in what she's singing and everything changes. She begins to belt out lines like, 'I am brave, I am bruised. I am who I'm meant to be, this is me.' And, 'I'm not scared to be seen, I make no apologies, this is me.' You can see her nerves kick in again as the song slows a little and she grabs her co-star Hugh Jackman's hand just long enough to remind herself she can do it, and then on she goes.

Diane showed me the video, and as I watched I felt God say, 'It's time to step away from the music stand.' I'm not the kind of person who feels like they hear God all the time, but it was such a strong impression that he was saying to me, 'The world needs you to be more you, to be the person I made you to be, not what you think others want you to be. Own your story, step out of the shame you feel and realise how much I love you for who you are.'

It was such a powerful moment but equally completely terrifying. God wasn't saying, 'You will now be miraculously unafraid of what anyone thinks of you, and everyone will respond to you in exactly the way you want them to.' He was saying I had to be more vulnerable. I was scared and didn't think I could do it. I've read lots of self-help books over the years and as amazing as they were and as moving as the clip from *The Greatest Showman* was, I knew I couldn't just muster up a sudden sense of self-acceptance and self-confidence.

Then the penny dropped. God wasn't asking me to do it in my own – very limited – strength. He wasn't asking me to do it myself. He was saying it's not just about *who* you are, it's about *whose* you are. We can't expect to get from ourselves or others what only God can give. As important as relationship with safe friends and individuals are, they will never be able to love us in the same way God does. Expecting them to do so will set us, and them, up for failure.

Being authentic, being comfortable in our skin and our own story, comes from a place of knowing who we are as a child of God. You belong to him, you are loved, you are of great value. When we know this deep in our souls, then we know it is true, whether we're standing among lots of people who agree with us or disagree with us. We know it's true whether we feel like we have succeeded or failed. We know it's true on a good day or a bad day. The truth remains the same: you belong to the Father.

We see this so clearly in the life of Jesus, who spent lots of his time disappointing people. Isn't it odd to think of it like that? Jesus, who was perfect, left many disappointed. So many had expectations of who he should be and how he should behave and yet he never wavered and bowed down to the weight of that. He withdrew from crowds who were desperate for him, he slept while his disciples were facing a huge storm, he was friends with prostitutes and tax collectors, he didn't keep the Sabbath as the Pharisees understood it, he wasn't the military Messiah many had been praying would come and defeat the Roman Empire. The list goes on. If he'd tried to keep everyone happy he'd have achieved nothing; instead he lived to please his Father. He didn't have to do anything to earn the Father's love, that was already his. In Luke 3:21–22, we read about Jesus' baptism and that God ripped open the heavens to say, 'You are my Son, whom I love; with you I am well pleased.' I love the word 'ripped'; it implies that it will never be the same again, an echo of the way Jesus was crossing the divide between heaven and earth. Of course, Jesus hadn't done anything at this point in terms of ministry; he was loved for who he was not what he did.

Ministry leaders, Steve and Chris Hepden, write, 'The Father was pleased because of who Jesus was, not what He was going to do. No wonder Jesus felt safe as He went out in the towns and villages of Israel. He knew who He was and was secure enough in Himself and His Father's love to go and fulfil His calling.'[14]

As I tried to take hold of God's encouragement to me to step out from my hiding place, my place of security, I realised that ultimately there is only one person who gets to say if I am worthy: God. A major difference between this book and a self-help book is that I'm not suggesting we look inside ourselves and muster up the strength to love ourselves. We are loved because of who Jesus is and what Jesus did for us; we are defined by the love he showed for us on the cross. As I said, it's not just a case of being comfortable with who we are; it's holding on to the truth of whose we are. We belong to God. We're his idea, his creation, his design, his beloved. That's true for each and every one of us, no matter how we feel, no matter what we've done or not done. It's true because he never changes.

ELLEN'S STORY

Ellen and I were part of a church plant in East Peckham, London, and I have always been inspired by her heart for justice and her servant attitude, working alongside vulnerable young women to show them God's love in action. Ellen, and her husband Phil, moved to Brighton, so I have not seen them for a while, but when I was praying about this book, I knew I wanted to get in contact and ask them if they would be willing to tell their story. They are amazingly resilient and I know their story will speak to many.

The hardest words I've ever had to hear were delivered when I was 18-weeks pregnant. The sonographer looked at me and said, 'I'm really sorry but your baby has no heartbeat.' In that moment, a pain ripped through me like nothing I'd ever known. I felt like I was falling off a cliff.

There had been so little warning. My husband, Phil, and I had been blessed with two healthy children. Both times the pregnancies and the labour had been relatively straightforward and the ease of the whole process added to our naive view of life that if you wanted to have a child it was likely to happen. I knew that miscarriages and stillbirths occurred, but after two pregnancies I wasn't unduly concerned about it happening to me.

We'd been married for four years when Eva was born

in 2009. She was a contented, dark-haired bundle of goodness and we loved becoming parents. Two and a half years later Jonah joined us, and he brought further joy to the family. Life was hectic but fun, balancing the changed demands on our time with the joys of bringing up two children. Phil and I were both passionate about our work too. I had trained as a counsellor and set up a charity providing therapy for survivors of sexual abuse as well as new mums suffering from postnatal depression and anxiety, while Phil worked as an accountant for Christian charities.

To many, it seemed our family was complete, with one girl and one boy, but we couldn't get away from the idea of having a third child. I am one of three siblings and Phil is one of five, so it seemed natural to us to have a larger family.

As I approached 40, the question became more pertinent: would we try for a third baby? Eva was 9 and Jonah almost 7, so life had found a more established rhythm. It had been a while since we'd thought about sleepless nights and nappies. Though we'd enjoyed having a bit of our independence back, the desire for a bigger family hadn't gone away. Phil and I talked it through and felt we would really regret not trying. We knew there were more risks given my age, but as everything had been straightforward in the past we weren't too worried.

We were on holiday in a little caravan in Brittany, France when we found out I was pregnant. The sun was shining and we'd headed to a French supermarket to track down a test to confirm what we already suspected. Phil and I kept this wonderful secret to ourselves, not yet ready to share it with Eva and Jonah. We were wrapped up in a blissful bubble, excited for the future and this next stage in our family life.

Back home in Brighton, I had some bleeding, which frightened me, but having called a midwife I was reassured that this wasn't uncommon and was unlikely to be a sign of any more concerning issues. The 12-week scan and all the additional tests confirmed that everything was OK, and we both breathed a sigh of relief. We started sharing the good news with family and friends, who were delighted for us. One of the most precious moments was sitting Eva and Jonah down to tell them they would be a big sister and a big brother. I'll never forget the joy on their faces. We started to plan in earnest about what life was going to look like, and our hearts opened to the joy of this new life. We had to get practical too; we knew we needed an additional bedroom so set plans in motion for an extension to our little house. As each week passed with no bleeding, I was reassured that everything was well. The house became chaotic with the building work but we all enjoyed making plans for when it was done and the baby had arrived.

Then, one morning, as I neared the 20-week mark, I went to the toilet and saw blood. Lots and lots of blood. I couldn't move for fear and cried out to Phil. A call to the midwife confirmed we needed to get to hospital as quickly as possible to investigate what was happening. The next few hours were a blur as we organised friends to take care of Eva and Jonah and rushed to hospital to begin a process of investigations. As we sat and waited quietly in the hospital tower block overlooking Brighton beach, I knew something was horribly wrong. The tests culminated in a scan to see if they could determine where the bleed was coming from. The world as I knew it came crashing down as we heard that sentence: 'I'm really sorry but your baby has no heartbeat.'

There was little time to process what we'd heard before the doctor explained that because I was so far along in the pregnancy I would have to deliver the baby. They wanted to start the medication straight away to get the contractions started. Through our grief, we knew we had to let Eva and Jonah know what was going on, and that we had to tell them face to face. They had been so excited seeing my bump grow and making plans for when the baby came. The doctors reluctantly agreed, giving us strict warnings to be back in the next couple of hours, and so we headed home.

One of the hardest parts of the whole thing was delivering that sad news to our children and seeing the grief and loss on their faces. They were shocked, and whilst Eva went quiet, Jonah connected with the unfairness of the situation straight away. 'It's not fair,' he cried out immediately. 'Why did it have to happen? I'm so angry.' His words felt like those buried deep inside our hearts, ones that as adults we often don't know how to express. We stayed as long as we could but had no choice but to take them back to our friend's house and head to the hospital as the contractions grew stronger.

This time we went directly to the bereavement suite. It was a new addition to the labour ward, designed especially for people in our situation so that we didn't have to be surrounded by the cries of newborn babies. People often remark when they hear our story that delivering a baby you know won't live must be the hardest part, but truthfully for me, it was hearing that there was no heartbeat that split my heart in two. That was where the trauma was. Up until then, we'd imagined life with this new little one, speculating on whether we'd have a boy or girl, what we'd name them, whether they'd look like Eva or Jonah. We'd envisaged a life as a family of five. That was taken from us in an instant and I can at times still hear those terrible words ringing in my ears.

Of course, the delivery was desperately sad, and Phil and I cried the whole way through, but there was also something so precious and sacred about that night. We were on the 13th floor and overlooking the sea at sunset, the team looked after us so beautifully, sensitively speaking to us in whispers and making sure the lights were dimmed. The birth was given the greatest of respect and tenderness and it was remarkably beautiful given the heartbreaking circumstances. Once the baby had been delivered, we were told it was a boy; we'd chosen not to do a gender scan earlier when we'd been anticipating the joy of a surprise at the end of the nine months.

The bereavement suite had a double bed and we were given space to sit – me, Phil and our little boy. We spent the whole night with him, taking in every inch of him and saying our goodbyes. He was tiny enough to fit in the palm of my hand but he seemed perfect, his fingers and toes all perfectly formed.

The team who cared for us were incredible; it felt like they were angels who anticipated our needs and gave us the kindness, time and space we needed. But after 24 hours in the suite it was time to hand over our little boy and our hearts ripped open. I have never felt so raw in all my life as a flood of emotions rolled in, overwhelming us both – the shock, the loss, the grief of saying goodbye to our son before he'd even taken a breath. We had to leave the hospital with empty arms, and as we walked out of the suite we were so blinded by grief and tears we couldn't work out where the lift was. The emptiness almost took my breath away. A midwife heard our tears and came out to help us, taking hold of my arm and leading us through the rabbit warren of a hospital. It felt like God's gentle hand guiding us and showing us his kindness while we were engulfed by grief.

We wanted to give our boy a name, one that acknowledged the weeks I carried him inside me, and the hope and the joy that he'd brought us in that time. We settled on Jesse, which means 'God's gift'; he still felt like a gift to us even in our pain, and he still does.

We constantly asked ourselves and God why, why, why this had happened. Though Jesse was given a post-mortem, there were no answers. We were left with the difficult conclusion of 'unknown loss'. In those first few weeks when the grief was like a thick fog around us, we planned a cremation and funeral so we could say goodbye, writing a short service to express our love for him.

The day of Jesse's funeral was cold and wet. The only time the rain stopped all day was when we were in the chapel. Walking in and seeing the tiny coffin before us broke our hearts all over again, imprinting an indelible memory on us. We lit candles to honour Jesse's short life and we felt such a feeling of love around us both from those in the room and from God. A rock-solid love that held us up and kept us going. Later that day, a friend messaged me and told me while we were inside for the service a beautiful rainbow had appeared across the sky. It felt like God's promise of hope that we would find a way through the pain.

I tried to hold on to that hope, though I found myself battered time and time again with waves of grief. Without warning, a wave would pull me under like a riptide, swamping me and leaving me gasping for breath. The emotions were so intense and I never knew when the next wave would come; sometimes they seemed continual. It was just a few weeks till Christmas, a season I'd expected to experience with a swollen stomach, and instead I was empty. We braved a Christmas service, wanting to connect with God in our pain. The chosen text was Luke 1, when Elizabeth sees Mary and John the Baptist leaps in her womb. I rushed out in floods of tears. With the whole Christmas story being about God being born as a baby, there was little that didn't feel too painful for us in our raw state. It was hard to fit in with celebrations with family and friends too; we were in no place to celebrate. Instead of our usual extended family gatherings, some family friends came to be with us. They didn't try to cheer us up or push us to a place we weren't ready to be, they simply came to be with us as we were. It was the greatest gift.

New Year felt like a huge hurdle. We'd thought 2019 would be dominated by our new arrival and instead it was a blank sheet. Phil returned to work after compassionate leave and Eva and Jonah had to go back to school; life had to carry on.

In January, a deep depression set in. Everything felt so bleak. I knew how much I had to be thankful for. Eva and Jonah ensured life went on and I was more thankful than ever that they were healthy. A few times people said about Jesse, 'At least you have two children already.' I knew where they were coming from, but it was still like a knife to my gut. It hurt to think that Jesse's life and loss didn't count because we had two children. Grief can be so lonely; well-meaning comments like that can make you want to hide away in your pain rather than reach out and risk being misunderstood and hurt.

I felt so lonely and isolated, but I knew early on that

I couldn't journey my grief without others around us. I feared some would avoid us as they didn't know what to say, especially as there is so much taboo around baby loss. I posted on Facebook that we'd lost Jesse, so people would know they could talk to us about him and help us through those dark days. This is what I wrote:

Dear friends

On Monday night I gave birth to a beautiful baby boy. He was perfect, but it was far too soon, and his heart had stopped beating sometime inside me, and he was already gone. We named him Jesse, which means 'gift from God'. We got to spend a night and day with him, which was both desperately sad and deeply precious, before we had to say goodbye. All of us are heartbroken – we all wanted him so much. To everyone who has so kindly asked us what you can do to help, what we would ask is please don't tiptoe around us in the coming weeks. We very much welcome people around us, asking us how we are doing, showing us care, helping us keep the memory of Jesse alive. We would rather have a really awkward conversation with you, where neither of us knows what to say, but we are trying to be real and honest, rather than ignoring this overwhelming grief we feel. And if it really is too hard to find words, which it will be at times, just hug us. We can't thank all our family, friends and medical

> staff who have walked these last few days with us
> enough. We are being held up by a tidal wave of
> love which is all around us – we are so grateful.
> Ellen, Phil, E & J xx

It felt so vulnerable putting that out there, but our friends and family were amazing. A tsunami of love came towards us. Yes, people fluffed their words, but they tried and that meant the world to us. They did their best to understand what we were going through and made us feel loved with their hugs, meals and flowers. I knew I needed a big support network, so as well as talking to friends I started seeing a counsellor and a spiritual director. It was like building scaffolding around me to keep me from crumbling. One of the key things I know about resilience is that asking for support is a strength not a weakness. I wasn't going to make it without people around me.

I also needed to be kind to myself. I went through a phase of self-blame, where I questioned everything. I wondered whether I'd taken a bath that was too hot or if dyeing my hair had caused damage to Jesse; I examined and re-examined every little thing, looking for clues as to why it had happened, convinced it was somehow my fault. I felt like a failure; embarrassed and ashamed that I hadn't been able to carry my baby to term. Instead of turning on my body, I needed to help it heal, so I found a massage therapist who specialised in traumatic experiences. As she soothed the aches and pains from the muscles, I found a place of peace where I could start to forgive my body. I had friends and medical professionals who told me it wasn't my fault and that was something I desperately needed to hear to stop me being engulfed in guilt and shame.

I knew I couldn't return to my job as a counsellor so I decided to go to college and train to be a florist. I had done some introductory courses previously and thought that working with flowers would be soothing and would ground me in the here and now. Our church has a therapeutic farm, so for months I spent time growing flowers and tending to them, then taking them to a market to be sold. The depression had been overwhelming and I needed to be around life and beauty again. There's something so hopeful about planting a seed, knowing it will grow and watching the cycle of life begin. It was soothing to get my hands in the dirt whilst growing beautiful flowers and feeling the sun on my face as I tended to them.

While we knew we needed time to process our grief, the doctors had made it clear to us that if we wanted another child we couldn't afford to hang around for too long because of my age. They said that losing one baby wasn't an indicator that we would lose another. We also had to make a fairly quick decision around whether we wanted to try again for a baby, and we decided we really wanted to. Amazingly I got pregnant quickly and a wave of hope rose in my heart, but the fear was still present. Now that we knew first-hand just how horribly wrong things could go, we'd lost our naive optimism that it would all be OK. The hospital provided extra support because of our circumstances and we had an early scan at eight weeks. There we heard those awful words again: there was no heartbeat. Loss compounded loss and it was a struggle to breathe.

There was nothing the hospital could do for us; we were sent home and told I would miscarry naturally. Eva and Jonah were adamant that the baby should be named even though it was too early for us to tell if it had been a boy or a girl. Together we chose Winter as a gender-neutral name.

The emotions were so strong I felt like I was being pulled under. Depression. Grief. Sadness. Anger. Why us? Why had we lost two babies? We wanted them so very much. I went to my GP and began talking anti-depressants to try to get on top of the hopelessness that had overtaken me. Around us, it seemed like everyone was getting pregnant and having babies; being part of a large church means it's a fairly constant occurrence. It was a continual reminder of our loss and I feared this would be the end of our family's story. I knew that God could handle my anger though, so I let rip at him. I was like a child thrashing in their parent's arms, hysterical and overwhelmed but held in love. When we supress anger it can fuel depression, so I wanted to release mine in the safest way possible: into God's loving arms.

We were so thankful for people who continued to journey with us and let us be as we were, people we could be honest with that we weren't OK. Grief is a journey and it sometimes felt like people were waiting for us to arrive at the destination of healing and 'move on'. As time goes by, people expect you to be over it and stop talking about it. I had to learn that there was nothing wrong with me for what I was experiencing. I realised you don't 'get better', 'move on' or 'get over it', you just learn to live with the pain and in time the pain lessens. It will never feel OK to me that my two longed-for babies died, but I have learned to accept that it is the reality I am living in.

Some people find they can't talk about miscarriage and baby loss at all, and we had our eyes opened to the number of people who suffer in silence. In the weeks after losing Jesse and Winter, we had numerous cards, texts and whispers from friends telling us they had been through something similar. We'd had no idea. Often when a miscarriage occurs in the early weeks, people don't tell anyone because no one knew they were pregnant. So many suffer in silence. Because I was 18-weeks pregnant with Jesse, our loss was visible; we couldn't have hidden it even if we wanted to. Phil and I both felt strongly that we wanted to speak up, especially to support others who had been through something similar.

Thankfully we also knew we could bring our messiness to God. In our grief, we didn't feel like we had to get ourselves together, put on a brave face and pretend everything was OK. We were raw with God, not hiding anything and crying out to him in our pain. Our prayers may have been no more than silent cries, but they were real and we know they were heard. We didn't know what would happen next or where our story would lead us. We had no promise from God that we would get a longed-for third child, and even if we did, we knew they wouldn't replace the children we'd lost. Grief doesn't work like that. All we could do was look at each potential ending in the eye and say, 'God, would you help us whatever happens?'

Phil and I decided to have some counselling together, and by the summer it felt like there were more calm days on our sea of grief than stormy ones. Some of the rawness and intensity had faded. It would still have the power to take my breath away, but it wasn't such a constant onslaught and I had times when I could breathe more easily.

By July, Phil and I agreed to try once more. We knew if anything went wrong this time we couldn't handle any more grief and we would stop. We had great faith in God's goodness but knew that didn't guarantee us a happy ending.

We found out we were pregnant in August but this time instead of the blissful bubble of joy we'd experienced in France, we found ourselves filled with anxiety. We were truly thankful for the new life forming but aware of the fragility and scared that at any minute things could change. Every time I went to the toilet I looked for blood. Day after day, week after week of constant checking, each time holding my breath, preparing myself for what might happen. The hospital team were great, providing us with extra support and scans to keep an eye on the baby's development. Each time we had a scan, Phil and I braced, waiting for terrible news. Each milestone we got through gave us another tentative reason to hope. As we approached the final trimester, something happened that no one had expected: a virus swept the world, creating havoc like no one had known before. COVID-19 changed everything. I was already petrified about giving birth and suddenly all bets were off. It seemed like no one knew what was going on and policies were having to be created as the situation developed. My anxiety was sky-high not knowing what would happen. I was due to have a planned C-section as the baby was breech and, as the country went into lockdown, I went into hospital, alone. To try to minimise the risks and exposures, Phil wasn't allowed to be present at the birth. While I have never been so terrified, I experienced the peace of God surrounding me. I lay on the operating table and it felt as though I didn't take a single breath until I heard the cries of our little girl. She was here! She was safe! As a midwife handed her to me with a smile, a sob came up from my core. I was flooded with relief, with thankfulness, with the greatest love for my daughter, and once again with the loss. I sobbed for the joy of Ivy's life and I sobbed for the loss of Jesse and Winter. I wished I could have embraced them like I could embrace Ivy. I wished I could have heard their cries, seen them open their eyes, felt the warmth of their skin next to mine and looked into the future together.

We've known God so close in our grief. You imagine that when something devastating happens it might cause you to turn away from God or lose your faith, and yet the opposite has been true. We've learnt that God understands our broken hearts and holds on to us when we're in pain. We knew God wanted the best for us but that didn't mean he'd promised us a healthy baby. We've had to live in the uncertainty, walking day by day holding on to God, holding on to each other and being held up by those around us. We had to choose to show our vulnerability, to take risks even in our pain, to be kind to ourselves and to accept the painful reality of our loss while holding on to the truth that we have always had so much to be grateful for.

CHAPTER 3

GROWING THROUGH PAIN

Every time I had a conversation with someone about resilience, the name of one book seemed to pop up: *Option B: Facing Adversity, Building Resilience, and Finding Joy*. It's written by Sheryl Sandberg, the chief operating officer of Facebook, and tells her story of the aftermath of losing her 47-year-old husband. Sheryl and Dave were on holiday with friends in 2015 when Dave died suddenly of a cardiac arrhythmia. There were no warning signs and no second chances; he couldn't be revived. At the age of 45, Sandberg found herself a widow and single mother of two small children. Somehow, she had to get herself, and them, through these agonising unchartered waters. Shortly after his death, Sandberg was talking to a friend about an upcoming father-child event and who should go. She said that, of course, what she wanted was for her son to be able to go with his dad. Her friend told her, 'Option A is not available. So, let's just kick the s--- out of option B.'

I found her story incredibly inspiring, and one of the

things that spoke to me was when she wrote about the work of psychologist Martin Seligman, who spent decades studying how people deal with setbacks. '[He] found that three P's can stunt recovery: 1. Personalization – the belief that we are at fault, 2. Pervasiveness – the belief that an event will affect every area of my life and 3. Permanence – the belief that the aftershocks of the event will last forever.'[1]

PERSONALISATION – THE BELIEF THAT WE ARE AT FAULT

My 'all or nothing' personality can be a real positive. I meet challenges head on, I'm passionate, driven and I take responsibility very seriously. The flip side to that is I have a habit of taking on complete responsibility for things I can't control. When something doesn't work out as I think it should, whether that's in my role as a husband, a dad, a son, a friend or a boss, I can often decide to blame myself entirely. Taking appropriate responsibility is a good thing; taking over responsibility is dangerous.

I find this especially difficult with parenting my children. If one of my kids is struggling with English, I think it's my fault for not spending more time reading with them. When it's maths, I blame myself that I'm not smart enough to help them figure out the problem. If one of them is struggling emotionally, I wonder if I told them that I love them frequently enough. If they are struggling spiritually, I question if I have prayed for them enough. And so it goes on. At work too, I would blame myself for every failure and even every perceived failure. In the early days of XLP, when a team member wanted to leave their role, I would take it so personally, when in reality it was nothing to do with me, they just wanted to develop their career in a different direction.

I still believe in taking responsibility for our actions, but I've also had to realise that there are many things that are outside of my control. As human beings we will fail, make mistakes and let people down, but if we aren't careful we can start to see everything through the lens of failure. It's all our fault. If a relationship breaks down, we can think it's solely down to us. If we can't find a partner, we think we're not good enough. If we can't have children, we can hold a core belief that we are not woman/man enough. If we have children and they struggle in life, we must be the ones who did something wrong. In each of these circumstances there can be many other things at play.

Sandberg talks about a young woman who had been raped by a colleague, who blamed herself, saying it was her fault for giving the man a lift home. Rape is, of course, never the victim's fault and Sandberg was able to encourage her to see that what she did was an entirely reasonable gesture; the responsibility lay entirely with the man who raped her. Not everything in our life is a result of our choices.

When we do make mistakes, it's key that we keep them in perspective. Psychologists point out that we often jump from failing at something to calling ourselves a failure. A project, a dream or a relationship may have failed but that doesn't mean we should give ourselves the title 'failure'.

We make a mistake and call ourselves an idiot, when all we did was a normal, human thing because we're not perfect. We need to take appropriate responsibility for situations and learn from our mistakes so that we can grow, rather than sticking ourselves with heavy labels that won't serve us well in the future.

PERVASIVENESS – THE BELIEF THAT AN EVENT WILL AFFECT ALL AREAS OF OUR LIFE

After my limb reconstruction surgery, I lost my independence. I couldn't walk unaided and I couldn't drive. I couldn't get on the floor to play with my kids or allow them to clamber over me like they would have done before. Having a shower was a real challenge and I often needed Diane's help to do the simplest of tasks. Straight after the operations, I even had to rely on her to get me to the bathroom. I lost my ability to concentrate and my brain seemed incapable of holding on to a thought for more than a few moments. Even watching an episode of a favourite show felt too much. It seemed like everything had been taken from me and that the impact of the operations had touched every part of my life.

Reflecting back, I can see why it was so hard and why it felt like that, but I can also see that it wasn't actually true. It didn't impact *every* area of my life. I still had my marriage – Diane was amazing and looked after me and helped me throughout. I still had caring parents, in-laws and siblings, and my own children hadn't gone anywhere. I could still communicate with friends and work via text and emails. I was still loved by God even when it felt like he was being silent.

There were so many things outside of my control but there were also many vital, life-giving things still there. When coronavirus hit, many of us went through something similar. Suddenly there were all these restrictions and we lost so many of the things we previously took for granted: coffee shops, gyms, football, restaurants, playgrounds, being able to shop when we wanted and leave our house as many times a day as we liked. Even human contact was banished beyond the immediate home, which seemed the oddest thing to get your head around; even in times of war people still had the comfort of hugging someone. We were all on edge, anxious about what was happening and what was to come. On a rare outing to the supermarket, I drove past our local Park and Ride and saw it had been turned into a morgue. The news was full of loss from around the world and the trauma of those seeing it first-hand, both as caregivers in hospitals and those who lost loved ones. While it felt like COVID-19 was taking over everything, it helped me to remember this idea of pervasiveness. Without diminishing the very real, very difficult and very unusual circumstances of the world, I started a mental checklist: I am still loved. I still have my family. I can still go to church even though it's online. Coronavirus affected massive parts of our lives, probably like nothing else has before in my lifetime and nothing else ever will. The repercussions will be felt for years and yet it still didn't and won't affect every single aspect of life.

It reminded me of those amazing words from the Apostle Paul, showing that he managed to hold on to this perspective: 'We are hard pressed on every side, but not crushed; perplexed, but not in despair; persecuted, but not abandoned; struck down, but not destroyed' (2 Cor. 4:8–9).

With life feeling so utterly out of control, I also found it helpful to think about what I could and couldn't control. Psychologists recommend drawing your circle of influence: you draw two circles, and in one you write all the things that are worrying you that you can control, and in the other you write all the things worrying you that you can't control. So, for example, with coronavirus, we could all take responsibility for following the guidelines, washing our hands and practising self-compassion. We couldn't do anything to control other people's actions, the evolution of the virus and the decisions of the government. Many of us got sucked into a vortex of the 24-7 news cycle, full of incredibly frightening things over which we had no control. That said, we could control how often we consumed news, and after a while it became clear that it was likely to be better for our mental health to take a break from the news and check in on it, rather than have it on in a loop in the background.

A professor of psychiatry, PTSD and resilience at Yale University School of Medicine said, 'Many, many resilient people learn to carefully accept what they can't change about a situation and then ask themselves what they can actually change.'[2] Conversely, banging your head against the wall and fretting endlessly about not being able to change things has the opposite effect, lessening your ability to cope.

PERMANENCE – THE BELIEF THAT THE AFTERSHOCKS OF THE EVENT WILL LAST FOREVER

The final of the three Ps that can stunt our resilience is permanence – the belief that aftershocks of the event will last forever.

I have found Cognitive Behavioural Therapy (CBT) really helpful at times. It encourages you to write down some of your negative thoughts, then to look at the evidence for that thought being true and the evidence of that thought being false in order to arrive at a more balanced view. I found this particularly useful around grief. As you can imagine, when Sheryl Sandberg lost her husband, she got stuck in a dark place. She felt like she would never be able to come back from there, but she found comfort in understanding that we are wired to recover. She says, 'A psychiatrist friend explained to me that humans are evolutionarily wired for both connection and grief: we naturally have the tools to recover from loss and trauma. That helped me to believe that I could get through this. If we had evolved to handle suffering, the deep grief would not kill me. I thought about how humans had faced love and loss for centuries, and I felt connected to something much bigger than myself.'[3]

I discovered how useful doubt is after reading *Benefit of the Doubt* by Gregory A. Boyd, where he writes about embracing a lifetime commitment to Christ in the midst of uncertainty. He explains that some of the most dangerous people in the world are the most certain, those who don't leave room for doubt. Many wars have been fought by those who have said they are fighting for God. Throughout history, some of our biggest mistakes have been made when we are certain we are right, and it's the same with our personal lives and our faith. 'The certainty-seeking model of faith leaves us with an inflexible way of approaching our beliefs and makes us vulnerable to various belief systems,' Boyd says.[4] I started using doubt in a positive way to challenge my beliefs systems. I started to use phrases like 'maybe, I might be able to' rather than 'I can't' or 'I will never be able to'. For me, this was a big step forwards. I was beginning to learn to doubt some of the negative thoughts that would appear which would say 'nothing will change', 'that's just the way you are', 'you can't teach an old dog new tricks' and 'I will feel this way forever'. When you are in a challenging season, you feel that season will never change, but hope is saying, 'everything passes, nothings last forever'.

FIXED MINDSET OR GROWTH MINDSET

Psychologist Carol Dweck talks about the huge impact our mindset has on our ability to persevere in life using the terms 'fixed mindset' and 'growth mindset'.

Having a fixed mindset is when we believe that:

- our abilities are unchangeable;
- failure is permanent;
- critical feedback is a personal attack on us;
- it's not worth taking risks.

On the other hand, when we have a growth mindset, we believe that:

- we can improve through practice and patience;
- failure is a chance to learn and grow, to come up with new ways of and ideas for doing things;
- creativity and innovation are the ways to approach challenging tasks and so we embrace them.

Dweck comments that we often waste time trying to prove over and over how great we are rather than using that time and energy to actually improve. We try to hide our deficiencies instead of overcoming them. We look for friends or partners who will shore up our self-esteem instead of ones who will also challenge us to grow. We try to do the things we've always done rather than seeking out experiences that stretch us. She says, 'The passion for stretching yourself and sticking to it, even (or especially) when it's not going well, is the hallmark of the growth mindset. This is the mindset that allows people to thrive during some of the most challenging times in their lives.'[5]

When I first started reading about this, it sounded great in theory but I wondered if it was actually possible. Then I heard about Viktor Frankl, a psychiatrist who was a prisoner in a Nazi concentration camp during the Second World War. He went on to write a book called *Man's Search For Meaning*, exploring what it means to live a meaningful life. He wrote, 'Between stimulus and response there is a space, in that space is our power to choose our response. In our response lies our growth and freedom.'[6] If someone who lived through some of the worst horrors our world has ever known can say we have a choice about how we respond to life's circumstances, that carries some weight with me.

Psychologist Susan David describes this ability to put distance between our circumstances and feelings, and our actions as 'mental or emotional agility'. She says how we deal with our inner world of emotions and feelings drives everything, highlighting there is a conventional view of emotions as being good or bad, positive or negative, that is rigid and therefore really unhelpful when it comes to resilience. Instead, she encourages us to sit with our emotions, getting curious about what they are trying to tell us. She highlights that the more we try to ignore negative thoughts and emotions the stronger they become. Telling yourself to cheer up, crossly demanding, 'What is wrong with you?', denying the pain you are in, bottling it up or brooding on our emotions isn't helpful. Emotional agility recognises emotions as important signs – data telling us vital things about ourselves; it allows us to examine these emotions rather than responding straight away. We can then make a decision about which reaction we want to make that will lead us towards the life we want.

She stresses that the only thing that is certain in life is uncertainty and that we need to find a way to live with that rather than fight against it. As a child, when she was awake at night, scared of death, her dad would comfort her. Not with false promises that she would never die or experience the loss of anyone she loved, but by explaining that her fear was normal. What he showed her was that courage isn't the absence of fear, rather it's 'fear walking'.[7] Susan David says, 'Life's beauty is inseparable from its fragility. One of the greatest human triumphs is to choose to make room in our hearts for both joy and pain, and to get comfortable being uncomfortable.'[8]

Her insights particularly helped me, as I tend to react quickly to situations, thoughts and emotions as they arise. When I hold back and try to get the bigger view before I respond, I can see that my judgment is often clouded by past experiences and unresolved pain. When I stop to ask myself 'Why am I reacting like this? What is really going on here?', I come to realise that even difficult emotions, like anger, are trying to tell me something. Anger is often an emotional response to pain, and pain left unresolved can lead to depression and many other health challenges. I have found David's encouragement so helpful – that we should treat our emotions with curiosity, compassion and the courage to take steps connected to our values.

The only place I'd disagree with her is that, as Christians, there are a couple of key certainties in our lives: God's love, and his ultimate triumph over death. God promises to come and wipe away every tear, every pain, every depression, every cancer and trauma, every disappointment and loss, but until that day comes we have a hope that is real. Change is possible in the here and now. It may look very different to how we would like it to (I know there have been times when I've wished I could get some prayer and then leave church free from my anxiety forever). But God is always at work. He sees who we are becoming; he sees us with the eyes of restoration.

THE MINISTRY OF RESTORATION

Jesus had a beautiful way of seeing people's fragility and vulnerability and loving them rather than judging them for it. He saw the potential of what and who they could become. When a women was caught in adultery, rather than seeing her sin as the Pharisees did, he saw a child of God who had been abused by men and scorned by society. Rather than hitting her with the law and doling out punishment, he gave her dignity for today and hope for tomorrow. When he saw a man with leprosy, Jesus knew that he not only needed physical healing but also needed to be set free from the stigma that had dominated his life and could have determined his future. Jesus' ministry was one of restoration. Every time he embraced a person that everyone else thought was a waste of time, we are shown glimpses of God's intentions for human beings and a foretaste of the fullness of the kingdom of God.

If God is in the restoration business and I want to align my values with his and to do all I can to see his kingdom come to earth now, that means I need to remember that no one – even me – is a lost cause. God's kingdom isn't one that mimics the traditional power structures but is one built on vulnerability, weakness, grace, and acts of justice and mercy. It's through them that God's power is revealed.

Bryan Stevenson is a lawyer in the south of America who embodies to me this Jesus-like ability to see past someone's actions and see who God created them to be. He has spent his life taking on legal cases that no one else would touch, and his book about one such case (that of a black man wrongfully convicted of killing a white woman and receiving the death penalty), *Just Mercy*, has now been made into a film. In the book he says, 'Sometimes we're fractured by the choices we make, sometimes we're shattered by the things we would have never chosen. But our brokenness is also the source of our common humanity, the basis of our shared search for comfort, meaning and healing. Our shared vulnerability and imperfection nurtures and sustains our capacity for compassion.'[9]

You can see from the way he talks about the cases he's worked on that he sees each individual. He doesn't deny the need for people to take responsibility for their actions, but he also points out that there were often circumstances out of their control which led to tragedy. He reminds me so much of Jesus when he says this: 'If you take something that doesn't belong to you, you are not just a thief. Even if you kill someone, you're not just a killer.'[10]

He also reflects on his own brokenness in these moving words:

I am more than broken. In fact, there is a strength, a power even, in understanding brokenness, because embracing brokenness creates a desire for mercy and perhaps a corresponding need to show mercy. When you experience mercy, you learn things that are hard to learn otherwise. You see things you can't otherwise see; you hear things you can't otherwise hear. You begin to recognize the humanity that resides in all of us.[11]

American pastor and author Rick Warren describes life as railway tracks, with painful things and good things going along side by side. We all get some of each in this life, no one is just on the one track. But I also hold on to the fact that when we look ahead, right off into the distance, eventually the two tracks become one. The promise we can be sure of is that, one day, all the pain, the trauma, the injustice, the racism and the poverty will be gone and there will be only one track, where God restores this broken world to himself.

CHAPTER 4

LEARNING TO GRIEVE

We predominantly think of grief as being the agony of having someone we love ripped from our lives through accident or disease, but most of us will experience other types of grief too. For example, the loss of a dream can be particularly slow and painful, especially confusing if you felt like God had given you the dream in the first place. We may have seasons or even a lifetime where we lose our health or our freedom. We can lose significant relationships through a number of circumstances aside from death. All of these situations need to be grieved, and yet it's not something we're taught – or even encouraged – to do. We need to recognise grief for what it is in order to be able to deal with it. We need to give ourselves space and grace to lament that life isn't the way we hoped it would be. As a society, we often try to sweep grief under the carpet. Much of the time, we think we're doing well and showing resilience if we have the 'stiff upper lip' attitude, pretending everything is OK when it isn't.

We're not comfortable with showing others the extent of our pain or with seeing the vulnerability of another's loss. Perhaps it reminds us too much of life's fragility, and so we quickly turn away, hoping to stay immune. We try to give comfort as best we can, but what we offer are platitudes that 'time will heal', that the lost loved one is 'in a better place'. We can compound someone's pain when we pat them on the hand and tell them everything will be OK when they know the reality is that life will never be the same again.

When my brother Matthew died, at just a few days old, people tried to comfort my parents with words like, 'God must have wanted him'. My poor dad's response was, 'I wanted him as well. Why would God create him just to kill him?' I was young when it happened – in fact, it was the day before my third birthday that we lost him. For most of my life, I have struggled to celebrate my birthday, avoiding parties and big family gatherings. My birthday felt less like a celebration and more like something I had to get through. It was confusing having a celebration the day after the anniversary of something so painful for my whole family. I have no memories of Matthew, of waiting for his arrival, of meeting him in the few short days he lived or of the days that followed his death, but what I've always felt is an aching loss. A gap where my brother should be. A heightened nothingness. Grief has been there as a part of my family's fabric for as long as I can remember. And yet I didn't give myself any space to deal with my emotions. I pushed them down because it didn't seem like my place to grieve; that belonged to my mum and dad who had longed for and loved

Matthew with all their hearts. So I tried to ignore the pain I was in and then felt frustrated with myself when I felt sad that I had no brother to kick a football around with, or got angry when I saw other people with their healthy families, thinking, 'Why couldn't we have had that?' Of course, neither of those things helped, but I felt stuck because I had no idea how to express my grief in a healthy way.

Malcom Duncan, author of *Good Grief* says, 'Grief frees us from the servitude of our sorrow and gives us the ability to reflect on it, to enter it, and to exit it. We are able to experience it without being destroyed by it because through the process of grieving we are able to identify and learn to grieve. To put it another way, there is a point at which we can see our grief as part of us, but it is not the entirety of us.'[1]

More recently, I have made my peace with the fact that I will grieve for my brother until we meet again in heaven, because there is continued loss. As an adult, I've done a lot of work on grieving, but it's not like the loss stopped and then I healed and carried on. Everyone who has lost someone close will know that the loss continues throughout your life, every time there's an occasion that you wish they were at (whether it's as big as a wedding or as small as a family barbecue), every time you think of what might have been and what part they would have played in your life and in the lives of those you love. We need to learn to sit with our grief and to sit with others in their grief, not pushing down our emotions or trying to smooth over theirs with platitudes that have no hope of healing the gap.

A MODEL OF GRIEF

Many years ago, Elisabeth Kübler-Ross, a Swiss-American psychiatrist and pioneer in near-death studies, and author of the groundbreaking book *On Death and Dying*, identified the five stages of grief: denial, anger, bargaining, depression and acceptance. This shaped the way we have understood and explored grief ever since.

Personally, I've struggled with this model. I assumed I would journey through each of the stages until I arrived at acceptance. There I would be fine and whole. But I kept getting stuck on phases or feeling like I was going backwards. I got frustrated with myself for not being where I wanted to be or thought I should be. Grief isn't as neat as I had hoped! It's not something we can tackle by being proactive and just getting our heads down and getting through, reaching a magical 'other side' when we've put in enough time or energy.

Tanya Marlow is an author and speaker I admire hugely. She has had ME for over a decade and is only able to get out of bed for a few hours each day. Tanya recently pointed out to me that Kubler-Ross' stages of grief were actually what she'd witnessed in those dying, as opposed to those left behind when a loved one dies. Tanya said, 'Other grief is messier, it comes in bursts. It has its own timetable and doesn't fit with what we want it to do. We want to plough a line through grief but it's more like surfing; you've just got to keep afloat.'[2]

Another helpful illustration I came across was to hear grief described as a ball in a box.[3] Here, the idea is that the ball always stays in the box, where there is also a pain button. When you first experience a grief the ball can feel so large that you can barely move or function without it hitting the pain button. Many of you will recognise that feeling from those early weeks and months after a devastating loss; you can think of little else, and doing normal, everyday things that you took for granted before suddenly cost you more energy than you have. It feels like it will never change; it will always be there, consuming your every waking moment.

Over time, the ball seems to shrink a little. It's by no means gone, and every time it hits the pain button the agony is intense, but you can function a little more and the pain isn't as consistent. As more time passes, the ball gets smaller and the times of pain are less frequent still; they may still have the power to take our breath away but there is more time to recover in between each hit. For most of us, the ball and the pain never disappear completely and we carry elements of grief with us through our lives.

This illustration helped me see that instead of thinking of grief as something I could work through and come out the other side, my grief would change over time. Then, when I felt the intensity of loss, rather than beating myself up and thinking I'd gone back two stages, I'd realise I just needed to be gentle with myself.

A GRIEVING NATION

Tanya Marlow describes grief with a capital G for a major bereavement and a lower case g for smaller losses, but she says that while one has more impact, the grieving process is the same. Often with small losses we don't recognise them as grief but it's actually really helpful to our healing process to be able to understand and label our emotions.

During the coronavirus pandemic, many of us felt like we didn't have a right to grieve unless we'd lost a loved one. But we had all lost something: whether it was a holiday, the comradery of our work colleagues, our income, our freedom to go out, or celebrating special occasions from the small to the once-in-a-lifetime. We couldn't even gather to mourn loved ones, as funerals were limited to only five people at one stage. As the theologian N.T. Wright said, 'We are lamenting not be able to lament'. We had to grieve normality, as life as we knew it had disappeared and we didn't know if we would get it back.

George Bonanno PhD, a psychologist who heads the Loss, Trauma and Emotion Lab at Teachers College, Columbia University, said that grief is both natural and useful in these circumstances. 'Grief is really about turning inward and recalibrating, and thinking: "This is not the way the world is anymore, and I need to adapt,"' he says. 'It's okay to feel grief over what we're losing. When we do that, it allows us to let grief do its job, so that we can move on.'[4]

He also talks about ambiguous losses, those that 'lack the clarity and definition of a single point like death'. Not having clarity can make it harder to move forwards. It is usually talked about when someone has a condition such as Alzheimer's disease, where they are physically present but no longer the person we knew, or in relation to the disappearance of a loved one, where there is no body to show conclusively that they have died. I also think this definition could extend to include situations like an undefined illness that may or may not get better, a longing for a relationship that could happen in the future but where there is no guarantee; or a diagnosis of 'unexplained infertility', where there appears no medical reason why someone can't get pregnant and yet it hasn't happened. There are many times in life that loss isn't clear cut but is nevertheless very real.

My family experienced this first-hand when my precious nan started displaying the symptoms of what went on to be diagnosed as Alzheimer's disease. She was one of the funniest and kindest people I knew. She had a beautiful faith in God, and each night would always kneel beside her bed and make her way down a very long prayer list. I have cherished memories of staying at her house as a child and being told to do the same. For ten years we visited, watching her memory deteriorate to the point of not remembering who we were. Whereas once her face would light up when her children and their spouses or her grandchildren walked into the room, her eyes became lifeless and devoid of emotion over time. Seeing her became a painful experience, especially for my dad. There were times my nan would get violent and hit my dad, or become quite aggressive. It's so painful to lose the person you love while they are still physically there. There was the odd word she said, or the occasional smile that showed us a glimpse of the amazing lady we knew, but truly we knew we had lost her long before she died; we had to grieve that we would never have a meaningful conversation with her again. She was still very special to me, but, if I am honest, there were times when I was bit scared of her, when she was agitated and angry. I would then feel guilty for feeling that way as of course she couldn't help it. My dad visited her every week, showing her as much love as he was able and honouring all she'd done for him and the depth of the love they shared.

As she deteriorated very slowly, over many years, there was no moment I poured out my grief. Instead there were moments of denial that I would never experience that closeness with my nan again, and occasional times of deep sadness. When she finally passed away, the grief was able to find a focus and be released in a different way.

Friends have also described to me the loss of a dream. One friend longed to have children all of her adult life but remained single. Because she couldn't actively try for a baby, there was no obvious point to hinge her hopes on and no clear-cut journey for how to get where she wanted to be, or even if it would ever happen. There was no medical support, no investigations doctors could do to help her see if her dream would become a reality. Just a long wait to see if she met someone she wanted to start a family with.

She said, 'There were no landmarks and defined moments of grief, which made it really hard to process. Some days the pain was overwhelming and I'd find myself completely broken. Other days I was full of hope that it wouldn't be too long until my dream would be fulfilled.'

Though she was honest with close friends, to the rest of the world there was no visible pain or grief, which meant she'd often be subjected to difficult and intrusive questions. There wasn't a defined moment when people could rally round and comfort her in her grief; she says it was a slow realisation in her forties that it wasn't going to happen. 'Other than waiting for my body to be biologically incapable of pregnancy, I had to choose the moment to let go of the grief it was causing me to hold on to the dream. Friends often wanted to offer hope that it would happen, but I knew I was the only one who could decide when enough was enough. I'd grieved so much over the years that when I reached the place of accepting it wasn't going to happen, there was a sense of peace that came even within the pain.'

It's so hard in these situations to know when to let our dreams go and when to keep fighting for them. Not having black and white answers is so tough. The only thing I can come back to is I choose to trust, like the psalmist. I have questions and frustrations about things in my life as well as on behalf of so many people I love who desperately want to get married, or have kids, or to fulfil an ambition or dream in their work. I want to choose to walk alongside people as they make this journey and refuse to belittle their pain with pat phrases. I want to enter the mystery that God may well bring all of their hopes and dreams to fruition, while holding on to the fact that we live in a world of loss and pain, where things don't always work out how we'd want them to. Though I find myself continually frustrated by my lack of answers and lack of ability to change things for those I love, I want to choose to trust God with them. I want to wrestle with them as they seek God's wisdom for their lives.

A GOD ACQUAINTED WITH GRIEF

Wrestling with God is so different from serving up a Christian platitude. And we have a fair few don't we? When facing the pain of loss, I've had many friends say to me, 'Give your pain to God.' They meant it kindly, but it's not as if I have never thought of that or even tried. If we're not careful, the implication can be, 'Box up your feelings and hand that neat and tidy package over to God so you can get on with your life.' What I've loved instead is having Christians sharing honestly about their own suffering and what grief has done to them.

After author C.S. Lewis lost his wife, Joy, to cancer, he wrote about his battle with loss in the book *A Grief Observed*. It's a raw and honest journal, showing his questions for God. He didn't question that God exists but whether he is in fact good. He said, 'Not that I am (I think) in much danger of ceasing to believe in God. The real danger is coming to believe such dreadful things about him. The conclusion I dread is not, "So there's no God after all," but "so this is what God's really like. Deceive yourself no more."'[5]

Decades later, author Kay Warren coined a similar sentiment after her son Matthew completed a suicide at the age of 27. She said, '[When my son died it] felt like my faith had been reduced to ashes. I could walk away from God – but where would I go? It's not like the world has anything to offer. I was stuck with God, but he didn't seem like a very good option.'[6]

One hugely important aspect of both Lewis' and Warren's grief is that they both understood that God is good and that he can handle our questions. I don't think he's offended that we question his goodness when our world has fallen apart; I can't imagine why he'd have included some of the psalms in the Bible otherwise. We might have been tempted to only include psalms of praise and thanksgiving that made us look good; God in his wisdom chose to include those that asked 'Why?' and 'How long?' about the suffering the writers faced, as well as 'Why do you hide yourself in times of trouble?" (10:1) and 'Why have you forgotten me?'(42:9). In fact, 40% of the psalms are ones of lament. Old Testament scholar Daniel J. Simundson reminds us of this scriptural tradition, saying, 'The lament allows for honest interchange between humans and God, the freedom to admit even bad theology and hostile thoughts. The lament turns to God as the ultimate source of help and in the typical lament form, ends with the assurance that God has heard and will save. The lament does not solve all the sufferer's intellectual questions about the origin and meaning to the suffering but does provide a structured way for the faithful to bring their suffering to God's attention and to cope with it.'[7]

Author Kathleen O'Connor says, 'The point of lamenting is... to name injustice, hurt and anger... Laments empower sufferers to speak for themselves... Naming suffering before God reclaims human dignity and power that has been trampled and violated... Laments are the beginning of action, a rejection of passivity and so they can invert despair.'[8]

I love that emphasis on action, of actively engaging with our pain rather than trying to ignore it and hope it will miraculously disappear. Lament helps us to engage with God in our pain. It is an acknowledgment of the questions, the anger, the hopelessness, the frustrations, the grief. It's so important because it shows us how we can turn towards God in our pain rather than turning away from him. The alternative to engaging with God is that we absorb our pain, try to avoid dealing with it or find unhealthy cover-ups. These coping mechanisms only allow it to take root in our hearts and keep us from functioning the way we need to. We can harden our hearts, allowing anger to become a resident and not a visitor showing us there is something wrong.

The prophet Isaiah beautifully describes Jesus as 'a man of sorrows, and acquainted with grief' (53:3, KJV) – to whom else would it make sense to go in our own grief? A God who knows the sorrow of the cross, the sorrow of being rejected by the world he loves, is a God we can trust with our pain and questions. As we look to the cross we see he understands our grief. He doesn't understand it theoretically; he knows it through and through.

This came in to focus for me when I visited the 9/11 Memorial and Museum in New York, where 2,977 people lost their lives after the terrorist attacks on the World Trade Center on 11 September 2001. You may remember the photos from the time that showed a cross sticking out of the debris; a symbol of hope in a hellish wasteland. That cross was a 17 foot-long crossbeam, weighing at least two tons, and as you leave the museum it's the last thing you see.

Local priest, Father Brian, persuaded city officials to allow a crew of volunteer labourers to lift it out of the wreckage of the towers and mount it on a concrete pedestal. Each week in the aftermath of 9/11, Father Brian held services there. He became the chaplain of the hard hats, and whenever crews who were working to find the dead needed a blessing or a prayer, Father Brian was there for them. Sometimes victims' families came to pray, and Father Brian's congregation grew from 25 to 300 people of different religions, ages and races.

The priest says that in the days after 9/11, people were drawn to the cross as a sign that somehow death was not the final word. It was a place of lament, a place of questions, a place of what felt like unanswered prayers. There is surely no better place to ask questions than in the shadow of the cross, where you realise that God understands our pain, anxiety and confusion. Here we find our solace, that no matter how dark the day, no matter how painful the night, we do not suffer alone. Though we often wish God would just remove the pain from us, he never promises that until we reach heaven. Then every tear will be wiped away. For now, he promises he will never leave us alone. He joins with us, sitting with us in our grief, as our ultimate comforter and hope. He is our place of refuge when the world is too much. Psalm 46 puts it beautifully:

> God is our refuge and strength,
>> an ever-present help in trouble
> Therefore, we will not fear though the earth give way,
>> and the mountains fall into the heart of the sea,
> though its waters roar and foam
>> and the mountains quake with their surging…
> The Lord Almighty is with us;
>> the God of Jacob is our fortress…
> 'Be still, and know that I am God'.
>> (Psa. 46:1–3,7,10)

STEVEN'S STORY

I met Steven when he was 16 and I was working for XLP, the charity which I founded in 1996. Initially he was an angry young guy who was trying to deal with all that life had thrown at him. The change I have seen in him over the 14 years I've known him is remarkable. He has not only turned his life around with the help of XLP, he has also become a role model for so many young people. My kids adore him and his lovely wife Kaia and their little boy Malachi. He is my youngest child Caleb's godfather and very much part of our family. I could not be prouder of him.

My sister recently showed me a photo of me on my fourth birthday, when I was still living in Nigeria. I'm wearing the biggest grin as I stand proudly in front of my 'birthday cake', which is actually crackers and rice. The memories flooded back to me of feeling like I was on top of the world. Those crackers made me feel like I was the richest boy ever. It was only then, looking back at that photo, through my Western mindset, that I realised we had so little back then and yet it felt like everything. My two-year-old boy was sitting on my lap as I looked at that photo and I thought of the things we'd done for his birthday: the treats, the cake, the presents; I would have been horrified to serve him crackers and rice. But wealth is relative. We were 'rich' in our community in

Nigeria because we had electricity. We had enough money to eat, and our neighbours who weren't doing so well would bring a plate and a fork and come and sit and eat from our pot. To me, it seemed like we were doing pretty well.

I was born in Calabar in southern Nigeria. My dad wasn't allowed to be part of my life and I was never really told why. He'd try to see me from a distance, chatting to me from across the street when no one was looking, sometimes dropping money on the floor for me to collect. My mum moved to England, without me, for a better life when I was a baby; Mummy London we called her. She sent parcels home every now and again with designer goods in, letting us know about the riches of her new life. But I didn't know what she looked like till I saw a photo of her when I was 8. I stayed in Nigeria and lived with my stepdad and lots of siblings. Way too many siblings; my mum had a number of kids with a number of men, so it was hard to keep track of how many there were.

I went to church regularly and played drums there as a kid, but it wasn't a safe place. There was a hierarchy that I didn't understand. I read in the Bible that Jesus said the way to the Father was through him, but then the church pastor would tell us we needed to serve him and give him money to get close to God. It made no sense to me and I asked lots of questions to try to help me understand, but they saw it as a sign of rebellion and thought I was undermining them. I was forced to read chunks of the Bible and learn it by heart. I could have recited whole books for you but I had no idea what any of it meant. I had a faith in God but my relationship with church was messed up. The culture was more about worshipping ancestors and visiting witch doctors than it was about Christianity. But the darkness I saw all around me made me know there must be light too.

Some of my relatives believed I was possessed by demons – it was a culture thing. They tried to beat the demons out of me, starve them out and scare them out by leaving me in church for days at a time. They would always shout at me while they were beating me, trying to get me to confess things, but I had no idea what they wanted me to say so that would make the whole thing go on longer. It got to the point where they even put hot knives into my skin. The heat seared the skin, which stopped me from bleeding in the way they expected, but they just took the lack of blood as a further sign of me being possessed. They went off, talking about getting hold of petrol to douse me in. Strangely, I knew I would be OK. My sister was there, trying to comfort and help me, and I said to her, 'He's said I'm going to be fine.' 'Who?' she asked, confused because it was just the two of us left. 'That guy,' I said, pointing at what to me looked like a man but to her was thin air. Before my attackers could come back, my older brothers who lived nearby got wind of what these relatives were about to do and came to rescue me. They kicked out the family members who were hurting me and moved in themselves so I felt safer.

It's hard to explain the culture there because it's so different to England, and I know it sounds crazy. Death was a norm. Whereas here you might see the occasional dead animal by the side of the road, there it was fairly normal to see both dead animals and dead bodies. Death wasn't a big deal and we were all quite detached when we came across someone who was dead. 'I wonder what they did to not wake up?' I would think to myself, and then carry on with my day.

My mum came back eventually to get visas for some of us to move to England and be with her. It was the strangest thing to have a woman standing in front of you telling you she's your mum when you have no recollection of ever meeting her. There wasn't enough money to take us all, just the youngest three: me, aged 10, my sister, who was 11, and my 13-year-old brother.

We'd seen pictures of where mum lived. It was a housing estate in Brockley in South East London and she told us she owned the lot. In our minds, England was the land of milk and honey; we would pray in church that one day we could go to the place where the streets were paved with gold and we would see the Queen as we walked down them. I was so excited to start my new life in this amazing place with my rich mum. I was going to make something of myself and prove to everyone I was better than they thought I could be.

I realised mum had lied to us when she took us to her tiny two-bed flat. She was renting out one of the rooms so she could afford the bills, which meant my brother and I were in one room and she slept in the living room with my sister. It felt like being back home in Nigeria where we would have four or five of us sleeping on one bed.

We arrived in spring but I didn't start school until September. I was so confused when I got into the classroom; they were teaching us things I'd learnt years earlier in Nigeria. It felt like going backwards. The system was a lot less strict though; I couldn't believe the teachers wouldn't hit us. In Nigeria, the person who got the lowest grade in the class would get lashes, that's just the way it was. Instead, here, a girl was assigned to look after me and show me round because I was new. She was very needy and in my face all the time, hanging around and waiting for me if I went to the toilet. I couldn't stand the place and did everything I could to get out of school so I could be in the same one as my brother. I got into fights all the time, trying to make them get rid of me. Then I heard that another person in my class got transferred as he said he was being bullied. So I started saying the girl who followed me around was bullying me and making me nervous by never leaving me alone. My mum requested I move, so I went to my brother's school. I got my head down and tried to adapt to the new culture, learning new boundaries and trying to keep out of trouble. I wanted to learn, and I tried my best, but after a while I lost interest. I was re-doing subjects I'd already learnt and I couldn't be bothered to apply myself and do it all again. I got put in the middle or bottom set for each subject and I was bored. I didn't want to be a geek like the smart kids; it seemed to me the smartest people I knew were the ones who were dealing drugs on our estate. They didn't seem to have any problems in life, and they had loads of money. Everyone needs someone to look up to and the people we looked up to where I lived were the drug dealers. They would take people aside and give them £200 to take a package somewhere for them. It seemed like easy money. I was never in a gang but I used to do things I shouldn't have. I was emotionally dead after all the things that had happened in my life, so I just thought what happens, happens. I had no fear, just a survival mentality. If I thought someone was going to take my life, I had no problem taking action against them; I did what I thought had to be done.

Mum had lost her job and we were in some serious financial trouble. She was struggling but we weren't close, so it didn't affect me emotionally to see her crying. I couldn't understand why she'd left me for so long in Nigeria, and she just didn't feel like my mum. She would take us to the cheapest supermarket, Nettos, and make out that this was where all the superstars did their shopping. I hated that. She'd buy me shoes and tell me they were a good brand, then I'd get laughed at by the other kids, who said, 'He's got poor people's shoes.' It turned out the big brand names she'd sent to us back in Nigeria were things she'd bought cheap at a car boot sale in a private school. She made it seem like she had it all but it wasn't true.

The church we went to only made things worse. They would have 'prophecies' that someone in the congregation had £150 in their bank account and God was saying they should give it all to the church and then they'd get more in return. My mum would turn to me and say, 'That's me!' and she'd go and give her £150, leaving us with nothing to pay the bills.

Things were pretty desperate but there was one story that gave me hope: footballer Ian Wright had grown up on the same estate we lived on and he'd obviously managed to make a success of his life. I'd been into football too and I trained hard. It was my escape, my place of safety; whenever I had a ball at my feet the world seemed OK. By the time I was 17 I was given trials at a semi-pro team. It was on the way to one match after the trial that my sister called to tell me my dad had passed away. He'd been in a coma for days and she hadn't wanted to tell me because she wanted me to focus on the trials. They'd hoped he'd pull through and things would be OK but it wasn't meant to be. I didn't cry. I didn't even get angry. The manager asked if I was OK when I got into the changing room and I said, 'Yeah. My dad just died, but it's cool. We've got a game to get to.' The team didn't really know what to make of it but football had always been my escape. It felt like everything else didn't matter when I was on the football pitch and we won that game after my dad died 9–1.

By then I'd got involved with XLP too. I'd first come across them when they were auditioning people to be part of an MTV show called *Pimp My Ride*. They were turning an old police riot van into a mobile recording studio, and when I got picked it made me think I could achieve something. I was confused by Patrick who led the charity though; as far as I could see, he had everything – a house, a wife, kids – and yet he was still there helping other people. 'Why do you want to come and help kids in this area?' I asked him. 'Why wouldn't I?' he said. 'It's not about me. God loves you and I'm here to serve him.' It was such a change for me, going from pastors who wanted something from you all the time, to Christians like Patrick who were giving themselves freely to others. People who not only said that God is love, but lived that God is love. I started understanding that church isn't a building but God's presence is in his people. I saw that Jesus served his community and that we too should serve our communities. He didn't invite people who were homeless to come to him in a building, he went to them. I started to see that God was in the lives of people no matter their brokenness – it was like it was a beautiful mess that didn't put him off.

I felt like I came from a world where I had nothing and people like Patrick had everything. I thought they had no problems, but as I got to know new people I began to realise that wasn't the case, their problems just come in different shapes to yours. I had to learn empathy. Where I'd been so absent emotionally, I had to engage with what other people were dealing with, and I saw that their problems were just as real.

They might have had a stable family life, but they could still experience hurt and abandonment. They still knew loss and fear, they still had their struggles. I began to see that some of the things that had seemed little in my eyes compared to what life was like in Nigeria, were still big issues. Sometimes people would say what they were going through didn't matter because it didn't compare with what I'd been through, but I struggled with that. My story would seem little to people who have suffered worse. That's not how life works. We all experience hard stuff, just in different ways and in different times.

I wanted to be more like the new role models I saw and give to others, even if things were tough for me, so I started volunteering with XLP, working with young people like me who were facing similar challenges and who could so easily go down bad paths. I started to use my football talent to coach other kids, using it as a way to connect and build relationship, knowing that for many of them it was the same escape route it had been for me from my troubles. I started to learn that although it was easy to do the wrong thing, I also had a choice and could do something right. That felt powerful. I went on to do sports studies at college and now work fulltime for XLP as their Sports Manager, overseeing all the sports programmes. It's amazing to work with young people who come from similar backgrounds to me, where there are limited opportunities and young people aren't well supported, and to see their lives transformed. Lots of them have good intentions but they need some help with their execution and keeping on track. I've loved seeing different groups of kids come together and embrace their differences rather than using them as a reason to treat each other badly.

There are some amazing stories, like Lexus, who worked as my apprentice, who went on to be signed by Reading FC; and Reiss, who is currently playing for Arsenal. I'm always encouraged by young people who make wise decisions and work hard. Sadly, there are harder stories too. One lad I was working with had done really well and was about to start a coaching qualification, which would set him up for his working life. The day before his training started, a friend of his died, and everything changed. A series of events means he's now in prison awaiting sentencing. It's so hard to see things spiral because of events outside of someone's control. We still support him of course. No matter what. We have to show these kids that we care, not just when they're doing well but all the time; we have got to be there when people are down.

My life has changed so much but I've seen that racism has stayed the same. When I was younger I thought it was because I was a bad kid that I'd get stopped by the police all the time; now I don't know if it was because of the colour of my skin. I'm pretty sure if I was white I wouldn't have had undercover police officers following me from South London to Oxford Circus and back again, or telling me that I needed to go home when I was shopping in Chelsea when I was in my twenties.

When I was playing semi-pro football, I had a white man look me in the eye and say, 'We shoot people like you round here,' and another time someone got in my face during a game and called me a black pudding. One day while I was working at XLP, I left the sports field to run to the toilet and out of nowhere a policeman shouted at me to get on the ground. A white colleague came over and asked what was going on. 'I don't have a problem with you,' he said to my colleague. 'Just him.' He nodded at me. Recently a white guy told me racism doesn't exist in the same conversation that he told me he liked to fire black people from his company when he didn't like them. Each time I could have responded with anger but I knew that would only inflame the situation and make those people believe they were right and that black people are aggressive. I try to engage people in a conversation where I can, to educate them, and I walk away where I can't. I worry for my son though. He's boisterous, which is pretty normal for a toddler, but I know at some point in his life he will probably be judged for it and it will be held against him. I want to teach him to be able to articulate his opinions but I know that some will see him as rude regardless, just because of the colour of his skin.

All the hard things I have been through have made me a better person though, no word of a lie. Every single thing. I know that I don't need a lot to be happy. Life isn't about money and cars; if I had very little to live on I'd know how to make it stretch and it wouldn't stress me out. I know I'm blessed with all I have and I really appreciate it; the things I have now are the things I used to pray for. I always wanted to get married and have kids but wasn't sure it would ever happen. Now I'm a dad I just want my son to grow up in the most loving environment possible. My mum used to say to me, 'You'll be so wealthy but you won't know what love is.' I always thought that was true and it's taken me a long time to learn what love really is and to believe that people can love you unconditionally, not asking for anything in return.

As a dad I'm very protective. No one protected me, but there's no way I'll let my boy go through anything I went through. I'm constantly checking and vetting the people he's interacting with and I keep my eyes open for any harm that might come his way. When he falls over I try to teach him to get up so he knows he can always help himself. But I'm never far away. Whenever he falls and says, 'Daddy, hands' in that little voice, I'm always right there. I want him to learn resilience without going through any of the stuff that I did.

I don't believe we're born with resilience; I think we develop it from having certain life experiences. The CEO of a company has very different resilience to, say, one of my co-workers, because they have experienced different types of pressure. Four years ago, my mum was told it would be her last Christmas, but she's still here. She's in a wheelchair, she's had lots of strokes and she can't speak, but she's holding on. It's only now

I see how strong she is. As a child I didn't understand why she'd left me in another country. Now I see she was just surviving and was doing her best to play the cards life had dealt her. She got us out of Nigeria, away from the violence of that village and gave us an opportunity to have a better life. To some, having a house, a job, a marriage and a family is the norm, but I don't take it for granted. I had some pretty tough stuff to deal with growing up but I realised that these things happen – you can choose to complain or you can do something about it. You can make excuses and blame your parents or the government or your church or your teachers; or you can do something positive for yourself. You can choose to care for others regardless of what has happened to you.

CHAPTER 5

GOING BACK TO GO FORWARDS

We can make two mistakes when it comes to mental and emotional pain: one is that we refuse to take medication; the other is that we only take medication and neglect looking at underlying causes. Likewise, we can try to pretend that our past has no bearing on who we are or we can let it define us. Sometimes, to find healing we need to go backwards in order to go forwards, but this should be done with great care. Many of us have unresolved trauma from different stages in our lives and this can have a huge impact in the present with our emotional, mental and even physical health. Many of us don't want to look at stuff in our past; when something is traumatic, why would we be keen to revisit it? Sometimes we don't even realise it for what it is; it can feel like too big a claim to say we've been through a trauma, but I think this definition is helpful to make us see where we've experienced it in our life in perhaps less obvious ways: 'Trauma can be defined as any experience which causes the person to feel terror, powerless and overwhelmed and challenges their capacity to cope.'[1]

Trauma can have long-term effects, leaving 'an imprint on the person's nervous system, emotions, body, learning and relationships'.[2] As psychologist Bessel van der Kolk put it: the body keeps the score.[3] If we don't take the time to deal with our trauma, it can manifest itself physically in a number of ways.

In recent years, research has been done on how traumatic events in childhood impact us as adults, and the results are astounding. The research used the term Adverse Childhood Experiences (ACEs) and studied their impact on our future mental and physical health. The experiences include abuse (physical, sexual or verbal), neglect (emotional or physical) and/or growing up in a household where there are adults with alcohol and drug use problems or mental health problems; there is domestic violence, there are adults who have spent time in prison or parents who have separated. There are also a range of other types of childhood adversity that can have similar negative long-term effects, such as bereavement, bullying, poverty, and community adversities, such as living in a deprived area or a neighbourhood where there is lots of violence. Research in England suggested that 48% of us have experienced one or more ACE, with 9% of the population having experienced four or more. If we've experienced four or more ACEs we are far more likely to have a poor diet, smoke, have underage sex, be involved in violence, go to prison and use drugs. This then increases the chances of diabetes, cancer, heart disease and other health complications, which in turn put people at risk of early death.[4]

ACEs are not a destiny. If you're reading this and identify with a number of these circumstances, it doesn't mean you have followed this path or that you have to in the future. The more aware we are of the impact of such events, the more we can do to stop the cycle. The more we understand ACEs, the more we can help ourselves and others who have experienced them. They can help inform us about why we're acting in certain ways. We all form coping mechanisms over time, some healthy, some not. Kevin, who experienced a number of ACEs, including a home with domestic violence, living in poverty, and witnessing a knife fight at the age of four, said of his use of alcohol, 'When I drank alcohol, the best way I can describe it is when you're in a swimming pool and you hear all the noise and you jump under the water and it goes [quiet]... It was the most beautiful experience.'[5]

When we've experienced trauma, we often look for ways to muffle the noise and bring peace, but many of these coping mechanisms bring their own problems. They can often provide a short-term anaesthetic, but once it's worn off the original trauma is still there. For Kevin, it spiralled from drinking wine to trying marijuana, cocaine and methadone until he said he lost his sense of self, of who he really was. Whatever our drug of choice – cocaine, alcohol, binge eating, being a workaholic, getting lost in Netflix for days at a time, pornography... they all, ultimately, leave us empty.

So what are the healthy ways to deal with trauma? Like most things in life, there isn't a one-size-fits-all approach. We are complex human beings with very different personalities and experiences, and trauma can affect us all in very different ways. If you have experienced high levels of trauma, you may live on high alert all the time. It is exhausting because you're constantly stuck in the 'fight, flight or freeze' response mode. Some of us respond to trauma by becoming numb and emotionally distant but then feel shame for our behaviour. Post-traumatic behaviour can be puzzling to others, especially when it seems counterintuitive, for example, when someone returns to an abusive partner and puts themself in harm's way. It's easy for others to judge someone as 'weak' in those circumstances, whereas they have undergone changes in their brain which are then felt in the body.[6]

Trauma can have a profound effect on our hormonal, immunological and nervous systems. It can be like a smoke detector constantly going off. Smoke detectors are useful when there's a fire, but if they are going off all the time it is distressing for everyone around. Having worn a frame around my leg after my operation, I now physically react every time I see someone else wearing one. Likewise, walking into a hospital makes my heart race as my body reacts to returning to a place where it suffered trauma. I could relate to what Dr Bessel van der Kolk said around trauma being stored in your body. But when someone has been through ongoing trauma, it can rewire their brain to such an extent that they constantly feel unsafe and therefore live on high alert, even when they are not in any danger.

WHEN IT ALL CATCHES UP WITH YOU

My dear friend John Sutherland spent years witnessing trauma after trauma working as part of the Met Police. He kept going and going, until suddenly his mind started feeling cloudy, then he was exhausted, then he got physical symptoms of anxiety before he got swamped with a depression so severe he could do little more than get out of bed for three months. All the unprocessed trauma, that seemed as though it was just par for the course for those in the police, caught up with him. It's not uncommon for people to keep going and think they're OK through times of intense pressure and trauma, only to find it hits them once the adrenalin stops pumping.

For me, I'd tried to outrun various events in my life by working hard and getting on with it. But then, as I said in Chapter 1, I found myself in A&E with arm and chest pains that made me think I was having a heart attack. Much of what I needed to process was things like seeing the life drain out of my wife during an emergency Caesarean section where she lost almost three litres of blood. Because she was ultimately OK, and because she was the one who suffered physically, I had tried to supress how that made me feel. I wanted to be strong for her, and while that was the right thing to do as it was a hugely traumatic event for her, I also needed to receive support and be able to admit how utterly terrified I was. I thought I might lose her and I was completely helpless to do anything about it. I had been trying to cope for too long, burying emotions around similarly traumatic situations, thinking I was being strong. I had ended up feeling desperate and so alone in my pain. When a friend suggested I saw a Christian psychologist, I thought it might help and wondered why I'd waited till I was desperate to contemplate getting help. I walked into the first session with trepidation, determined we wouldn't talk about any childhood stuff and hoping that a magic wand would be waved to solve everything instead. I assumed there would be a prescription of Bible verses to read, some breathing exercises and an encouragement to get prayer. How wrong I was.

My psychologist helped me to realise that some of my pain had come from supressed anger. I was confused at the time, thinking I had nothing to be angry about. But like many people, I'd been scared of showing my anger over the years, had supressed it and now my body was telling me that I couldn't carry on any longer. I had lived through a number of traumas, as well as picking up a lot of secondary trauma from hearing other people's traumatic stories. Here in the UK, I've walked alongside mothers who have lost their children to gang crime, parents whose children died by suicide, young people who've been abused verbally, physically, mentally and/or sexually. I've visited places around the world where the trauma of poverty and violence is endemic, and spent time hearing people's stories. I've walked through the remains of blown-up buildings in war-torn countries like Kosovo, hearing from families who had to run for their lives when soldiers came. Seeing the fear, the pain and the devastation wreaked by these situations is hard to walk away from. I would come home, shaken and feeling helpless, but then I'd have to get back to work and family and all the other elements of life here in the UK with no space or structure to process what I'd witnessed and heard.

There were different exercises my psychologist tried with me, and some helped more than others, but, over time, I began to recognise the impact of being continually exposed to other people's trauma had had on me. I also realised that I took too much responsibility for others. However much I want to and however hard I try, I can't control how things turn out for other people. I am not their rescuer, that's Jesus, and he's more than capable of doing his job! I learnt a lot from studying the story of the men who lowered their paralytic friend through the roof to meet with Jesus (Mark 2). His friends were amazing. They really wanted to get him help, and get him to Jesus so much, that they weren't deterred when they found the house Jesus was in was full and they couldn't even get to the door. They literally ripped up the roof to get their friend help, risking ridicule and abuse from others who were there. They also risked the wrath of the people whose property they damaged; most theologians believe it was actually Jesus' home. The friends did their bit in getting their mate to Jesus, but Jesus did the healing, not them. It made me realise that while I want to change things for people, I can only do my part. I can carry my friend on their mat if they need it, I can dig up the roof that might keep people from experiencing God's love, but I can't force it. I can't do what Jesus can do. Taking responsibility is good; taking it too far isn't. When we're in the business of caring for others, which to a certain extent is true of all of us in the Church, we need to find ways to ultimately hand people over to God's care. We are called to carry one another's burdens, but that doesn't mean taking complete responsibility for each other. That's too heavy a burden to carry and it's a job that belongs to God alone.

Slowly, as I continued to see my psychologist, I began to process the anger that had been rotting away inside me. People can think you're courageous when you stand on a stage and talk to thousands of people, or when you go and mediate between two warring gang leaders. The truth is, being vulnerable with that psychologist, taking a look at the things that had caused me pain that I'd never dealt with, took all the courage I had. Each week, I'd try to think of a reason I couldn't keep my appointment, any excuse not to have to go back in that room where the focus was on me and my brokenness. There was no let up, no way of deflecting or diverting the attention elsewhere. It was just me and my stuff and no way out but through it. But honestly, the whole process made me feel so much less alone. No matter how loving friends and family are, we can struggle to tell them the whole truth about what we've experienced or what we're feeling for fear of them judging us, misunderstanding us or rejecting us. Or we often fear how hurt they might be to see the true extent of our pain or to understand where they may have played a role in our wounding. A therapist who is there just to listen, without judgment or control, and who can focus on you for an hour, is an absolute gift. Ultimately, my therapist made me feel safe. My feelings were validated but I wasn't left feeling helpless in their wake; I was given tools to process them and make decisions about how to move forwards. I have been on a long journey, which I am still on, and I'm so grateful my friend was wise enough to suggest I get some professional help.

A WORD OF WARNING

We need to be very wise in how we help people process their trauma, because sometimes digging around in someone's past can cause more harm than good, potentially re-traumatising them and causing serious damage. It's important that we are aware of our limits and don't try to take the place of professionals. This is perhaps especially true within the Church, where we long to help and see people come to a place of healing. We wouldn't expect someone who isn't a mechanic to start taking our car engine apart, just to be kind or because they were interested. In the same way, it is so important that we recognise and appreciate what mental health professionals can do. They have been trained over many years and receive ongoing support and supervision specific to their area of expertise. They are able to provide the support that we are not equipped for. That doesn't mean we don't have a role; friends, family and community are absolutely key in recovery from trauma and in resilience at large. We just need to lean on the professionals at times too and leave the complex work to them.

HOPE FOR HEALING

As well as hearing many stories of pain and trauma in my work here and abroad, I've also heard many stories of healing. One of our friends who runs a Kintsugi Hope group is Tony. He had a 30-year career as a police officer in Essex and dealt with many traumatic situations. He was beaten by a drunken mob one Christmas Eve, and during other incidents sustained a concussion, a broken arm and many bruises. Dealing with death, suicides, dawn raids, riots and losing colleagues all took its toll on him. Four times he did CPR in the hopes of saving someone's life, but each time it was too late.

Tony got to the point where he'd become station sergeant and, to the outside world, all looked well. But the build-up of so many traumatic situations, as well as the breakdown of his marriage, left him in a place where he didn't want to go on. He found himself on the seafront at 1am, alone in the bleak darkness, contemplating completing a suicide. He stood for a while, considering walking out into the freezing cold water, knowing he would die of hypothermia. Thankfully, as he thought about his two children, he couldn't do it and he turned around and went home. He didn't speak about that moment for 27 years but says, 'In the weeks and months following that incident, what helped me to get to a healthier place was my church house group.

They were incredibly honest, open and supportive. Though I never told them how suicidal I was, I did share some of my pain and my marriage difficulties. They listened, didn't judge me and they prayed for me. They, in turn, were vulnerable and open, sharing their struggles, and I realised that helping and supporting them helped me. Alongside keeping fit, sport, sailing, church and a supportive family, it all helped to keep the level of stress in my life from overflowing again.'

Another person whose story has had a profound impact on me is Alex. I met Alex when I was on a mission trip in Trenchtown, Jamaica, which is a place like no other. It's best known as the birthplace of reggae and the home of music legend Bob Marley. It's a vibrant community, but gun violence and gangs are woven in to the fabric of daily life. On my first visit, I was taken to Bullet Alley, where a number of young children had lost their lives due to a gang war. More recently, I visited a memorial to children killed in tragic and violent circumstances. Seeing their names and ages – some not even a year old – is heartbreaking. As you walk around you can often feel the tension in the air, knowing things could kick off at any minute, constantly reminded of the danger when you see buildings riddled with bullet holes.

On my last trip, I was introduced to Alex, who was five years old when he witnessed his father kill his mother. His father had accused his mother of being unfaithful, before he hit her in the back of the head with a rum bottle. Alex's father was sentenced to life in prison, so Alex was left without parents. His aunt took him in but found his behaviour was unruly and aggressive as he struggled to process the trauma he'd experienced. He would steal, get violent at school and break windows; he seemed out of control and his aunt didn't know how to help. Thankfully there was a guidance counsellor at Alex's school. His aunt said, 'I never knew how much she could help him. I don't know what kind of miracle she worked but I noticed that the rotten behaviour had completely gone. I recommend it to other parents now because it could mean they see a change in their child's life.'

The guidance counsellor used an approach called trauma-informed care, which means treating a whole person; taking in to account past trauma; showing compassion and kindness; and understanding the circumstances around an individual. It recognises that no one is born angry and if they are currently dealing with anger, there may be a number of factors at play that need to be resolved.

Alex's teachers told me the change in him was amazing, and it filled me with hope about how we can help. I've so often come away from these trips feeling overwhelmed and desperate, not knowing what to do about the number of guns on the streets, the poverty, the neglect of children, the sexualisation of young girls, and the fear experienced by the community as they lie in bed hearing gunshots outside their windows. But here was something tangible we could do: I persuaded my Kintsugi Hope trustees back in the UK that we should fund a full-time counsellor for the school in Trenchtown that we worked with, to help the children deal with all the trauma they faced.[7]

The counsellor uses play therapy and other techniques to help the children open up about what they've experienced, and deal with it in a healthy and safe environment. The reports from the school are amazing, with such inspiring changes happening in these kids' lives. Despite their continuing challenging circumstances, the children they work with are becoming role models for the young people in their community, and a number are going on to university, something that is extremely rare in that area. With the counsellor as part of the team, the school are able to provide more than education; they are providing love, care and community – a place where the students can feel safe despite the challenges around them.

FREEDOM AND GROWTH IS POSSIBLE

Talking about trauma can feel overwhelming. The reason why I wanted to tell you Alex's story is to inspire you that trauma is not a life sentence; individuals who have been through so much discover resilience. The reality is that, when given the right support and understanding, people can make the most amazing changes. I often find myself heartbroken and amazed in equal measure by the people I meet. I have been reminded so many times by the people I have worked with and continue to work with that there is hope. Recovering from trauma can be the toughest of journeys, but when we face our past with courage and with the appropriate support, we can often find it leads us to a place of growth. In fact, some studies have shown that

30–70% of trauma victims go on to report at least one positive change after the stressful encounter.[8]

Likewise, Dr Gregg Steinberg, author of *Fall Up*, comments, 'Tragedy doesn't have to kick your butt. Tragedy can lift you up, to take you to a higher existence.'[9] Many people who have suffered trauma go on to help others in incredible ways. We've seen it a thousand times played out on a national scale: people who have lost loved ones in tragic circumstances campaign for changes in the law so others don't go through what they have; people who have suffered set up charities to help others experiencing the same pain; families set up charities to honour their loved ones and continue the things they were passionate about. This doesn't quench their grief but it does allow them to look forward with positivity rather than to remain stuck in the past. For others, it may be that they grasp new opportunities in a personal or professional capacity following trauma, that they experience a heightened sense of thankfulness for being alive, or they notice an increase in their emotional strength and resilience.

As I've mentioned, Diane and I set up our charity, Kintsugi Hope, after going through a traumatic time. If it hadn't been for my operation that stripped back everything for us and left us reeling, we may never have become so aware of the need for better mental health support in churches and communities.

We'll go on to look at how we can find purpose in pain in more detail in the following chapter, but first I want to look at where God is in our trauma.

WHERE IS GOD?

Have you ever wondered what the Bible has to say about trauma? When you think about it, God doesn't shy away from it. In places, the Bible goes in to uncomfortable detail about what happened to individuals and communities; in other places, it uses poetry to express events we can only imagine. 'O LORD, heal me,' says Psalm 6, 'for my bones are shaking with terror. My soul also is struck with terror, while you, O LORD – how long?' (vv2–3, NRSV). They may not have called them anxiety disorders when the psalms were written, but the symptoms sound suspiciously familiar.

I wonder if over the years we've downplayed the trauma of the cross because it makes for such uncomfortable reading, but crucifixion was a hugely traumatic death. It's possible that the very prospect of it was enough to make Jesus sweat blood – a condition known as hematidrosis, which can be caused by extreme distress or fear.[10] The cross we wear around our necks as a symbol of God's love is also a representation of the cruellest instrument of torture. Theologian N.T. Wright says, 'If you had actually seen a crucifixion or two, as many in the Roman World would have, your sleep itself would have been invaded by nightmares as the memories came flooding back unbidden, memories of humans half alive and half dead, lingering perhaps for days on end, covered in blood and flies, nibbled by rats, pecked at by crows, with weeping but helpless relatives still keeping watch, and with hostile or mocking crowds adding their insults to the terrible injuries.'[11]

The former Archbishop of Canterbury, Rowan Williams, pointed out that the holiest place on earth was the cross, where our Saviour gave up his life for us. He said, 'The New Testament makes it clear in a number of passages that the crucifixion is in one sense the supremely holy thing – the holiest event that ever happened – and yet it's found outside the conventional holy places and a long way from conventional holy people. It's an execution machine on a rubbish dump outside the city wall. Holiness in the New Testament is a matter of Jesus going right into the middle of the mess and the suffering nature. For him, being holy is being absolutely involved, not being absolutely separated.'[12]

This always blows my mind. My idea of holiness was that it was about being separate, coming away, being pure and clean. But we find God in the midst of the trauma we face, not removed from it. His holiness means being involved. He doesn't always heal us as quickly as we'd like, but he never turns his back on us no matter what. When I talked to my psychologist about various traumas, she would ask me, 'Where do you feel God was in that moment you just described? Can you imagine him there? What would he want to say to you? What do you need to hear in that moment?' Each time, I found it so helpful to allow God to speak into those times of pain. In the moment it may have felt like he was distant, but of course he was always right by my side because he never leaves us.

As I look back, I can see that there is a rawness to my faith now that wasn't there in the past, an acknowledgment of the scars and the bruises and my inability to live on my own without him. In the past, I longed for noise so I didn't have to think about things that were painful; now I long for silence. My prayer is we will allow God into every part of our lives, instead of trying to escape, or numb ourselves. Then we will begin to see he is there.

Therapist K.J. Ramsey says:

> Suffering does not have to be a barrier. It can be a continual reminder that there is no part of your life where Christ is not present. There is no place too low for him to stoop. There is no place of your body too inconvenient for him to love. There is no place in your memory too dark for him to hold. There is no weakness too recurring for Christ to care for. He is patient, and he is present. Christ is holding us together by the power of his spirit, wrapping scarred hands securely around the most shattered pieces of our stories, carrying them with care because he chose to be shattered first, and placing them perfectly alongside his own into a mosaic of glory.[13]

CHAPTER 6

NOTHING IS WASTED

After I resigned from XLP, I crashed emotionally. I had spent 22 years pouring my heart and soul into the charity I had started when I was just 21, and now it was no longer my responsibility. Truthfully, there was some relief. My tendency to take on too much responsibility for everything and for everyone wasn't healthy. I'd carried the burden of keeping us financially afloat for over two decades, had felt the weight of keeping the staff team employed as well as happy, had been impacted by the secondhand smoke of being around so much trauma. On the other hand, I was bereft without it. I felt lonely and isolated. Whereas I had been part of a big team at XLP and enjoyed the camaraderie, I was now on my own. I had no fixed income and no idea what the future held, just a whispered assurance from God that he was calling me to something else. I became low, irritable and anxious.

While I was still at XLP, I had been invited to speak at the Christian conference Spring Harvest. As I found myself in the main venue on the final night, getting ready to speak to around 3,000 people, I felt God say, 'Tell people you're currently struggling with your mental health.' It was one of those moments where I definitely thought I had misheard. You want me to do *what*, God? How will that encourage anyone?

Over all my years at festivals, I had never heard anyone speak about their ongoing struggles with mental health on a stage that size. There might have been seminars that mentioned it or the odd speaker who referred to a mental health issue that had long since gone away, but never anything current. I looked over my notes. My plan had been to speak on humility, so I could see quite easily how I could fit in my struggles with anxiety. I stepped on to the stage, began my talk and, about halfway through, I took a deep breath. 'You guys need to know that I am struggling with my mental health right now; anxiety is very real for me.' I asked whether we, as the church, could stop preaching only the show reel of our lives, telling miraculous story after miraculous story of healing and wholeness, victory and revival, and start telling the other side of the story. 'Can we be honest about our struggles?' I asked.[1]

I finished by talking about shame, quoting Brené Brown: 'Shame loves silence, secrecy and judgment.' We step out of shame by owning our story. I asked people who wanted to step out of their shame to stand up. For a split second I feared that no one would and I'd be exposed and alone in my weakness. But, over the next few minutes, about a thousand people stood, offering themselves to God and asking him to meet them where they were at. It was such a moving experience as we all realised that we are so alike and we all struggle with similar stuff. Not talking about these things is not helping anyone, it just creates more shame, whereas honesty breeds more honesty and more freedom.

As I sat down afterwards, feeling exhausted, exhilarated and overwhelmed, I felt God say, 'I can use your pain; nothing is wasted.' After that talk at Spring Harvest, I received more emails than I've ever had from anything I've done, full of amazing stories of both pain and redemption. Some said it was the first time they'd ever heard anxiety spoken about without it being described as a weakness. Many of the emails described that night as a game changer, particularly those who were so low that they'd been contemplating completing a suicide. Bringing the subject of mental health out in the open enabled them to get the help and support they desperately needed.

I don't believe that God causes the pain, the tragedy and the heartbreak we experience in our lives, but I do believe that he can help us find some purpose in it. I know what I have been through has changed me and made me less judgmental than I was before. When I was a teenager, I remember my youth pastor doing a talk on fear and saying, 'Some of you are scared because you wake up in the morning, see a spot and think you have cancer.' That sounded like the most stupid thing I'd ever heard. Surely no one thinks that, I mocked silently. Now I can't tell you how many times I have Googled the most benign symptoms, convinced I have cancer. A cough. A cold. A tight chest. A headache. A stomach ache. Doesn't matter what it is, in my mind they all lead to cancer. Before it happened to me, I had no comprehension of how it feels when the fear takes over; your hands start to sweat and your heart starts to race. Though rationally you tell yourself it's just a cough, something so powerful inside is shouting at you that this time it really is serious.

The attitude I had as a teenager isn't that uncommon. Often people suffering with their mental health get blamed for their challenges, being told that they should just be more grateful/pray harder/pull themselves together/stop attention seeking/make better choices... The terrible list goes on. We would never do that with someone who had a problem with their physical health – in fact, we often think of people who have physical health problems as heroic for the ways they persevere. It's only in recent years that I've realised the disparity.

As I look back now, I can see how God has used what I've been through to make me less judgmental. Now I know not to judge what someone else is dealing with; they may not be dealing with the same thing as me but I can relate more easily. I can see that what I've been through has given me more compassion for myself and for others, and I've learnt so much more about God's love. I'd always been told that God loved me for who I was, not what I did, but it wasn't until I was forced to sit and do nothing because of the frame around my knee, that I could grasp it was true. I've learned about empathy as well – about rejoicing with those who are rejoicing, and weeping with those who are weeping (Rom. 12:15). Not trying to fix them or make everything better, but sitting with them in the good and the bad.

I continue to have anxiety but have come to a place where rather than just praying for a miracle, I'm learning to manage it. When lockdown began I feared I would spiral down, but the strategies I'd learnt over the years stood up to the test and showed me it doesn't have to be completely debilitating. Likewise, when my daughter Keziah needed to go to A&E the other night, I was able to bring to mind all the things I have learnt from writing these books and I didn't allow my brain to go to all the worst case scenarios it would have done before. While it has its challenges, I can see how anxiety can make me a better, more empathetic person, though I'm still getting my head around the fact that God is working in something as horrible as anxiety!

I remember one person saying to me after my operation, 'Stop trying to find meaning in your suffering. There is no meaning, you just have to accept that bad stuff happens and there is no reason for it.' I could understand where they were coming from, but I spoke to my mentor about it and he very gently said, 'Finding a little meaning is OK.' I'm not talking about a blithe 'everything happens for a reason' sentiment. Many of us know first-hand how damaging that kind of comment can be when something awful has happened. For me, I needed to hold on to the hope that I saw in the image of kintsugi art. I have to hold on to the fact that through my brokenness I have experienced God and he will do something beautiful in my life as a result.

POST-TRAUMATIC GROWTH

Most of us have heard of PTSD (post-traumatic stress disorder), which is where a traumatic experience leaves us with symptoms like flashbacks, nightmares, guilt, feeling on edge or isolated and withdrawn. But there is also something called post-traumatic growth, which resilience researchers describe as the way trauma and pain can leave us with positive effects. It can be defined as the 'experience of individuals whose development, at least in some areas has surpassed what was present before the struggle with crises occurred. The individual has not only survived, but has experienced changes that are viewed as important, and that go beyond the status quo'.[2]

Sometimes the terrible things that we have experienced leave us stronger, teach us important life lessons and shape our future. Though few of us would choose the path that includes difficulties – and of course we don't seek out adversity – we can come through it as a stronger and better person, recognising it can teach us things and help us develop.

At the end of every speaking engagement someone will come up to me to share their story; a story of disappointment, hurt and defeat. They'll tell me how they've seen, sometimes years later, how God used their heartache and turned it into something beautiful. I often struggle when they start telling me what they've been through; I find it confusing that God didn't stop their pain in the first place. But I also love hearing how God brings good out of even the darkest of situations, and am amazed at the human ability to keep going and find purpose in pain.

When we're struggling it can be helpful to ask, 'Can anything helpful or meaningful come from this? Does this nightmare have to end badly?' Author Chris Johnstone says, 'When we're in the depths of difficulty, it can be hard to see. But later we might recognise ways we can help people facing something similar, or play a role in preventing the same hardship happening to others.'[3]

Over the last 20 years I have spent lots of time with parents whose children have been killed due to knife crime. It's one of the hardest things I have had to do, as each child is a life that has been stolen, a family, a community and a school left devastated. One stabbing that was very close to home was that of David Idowu who was only 14 years old. He had done nothing wrong and just happened to be in the wrong place at the wrong time. The knife he was stabbed with was dirty and he lay in hospital for three weeks before his body succumbed to the infection. His mum, Grace, was devastated. She is also one of the most resilient and beautiful people I know. She set up the David Idowu Foundation, and started going into schools to talk to young people about the dangers of knife crime. The charity provides positive youth engagement activities to help young people stay away from gangs and crime. On the anniversary of David's death, I attended a memorial service for him. The front row was full of other families who had lost a loved one in a similar way. Each had lost a precious child; each had set up a charity or foundation to provide young people with opportunities. They had formed a real community and I was astounded to see how they had taken one of the most horrendous things you can experience, every parent's worst fear, and not been torn apart by bitterness, resentment or anger but had shown amazing grace, forgiveness and kindness.[4]

It wasn't the trauma of their loss that caused these positive things, rather the way they responded to the trauma. Their response doesn't minimise their loss and the impact the trauma of losing a child has had on their lives. Growth doesn't mean everything is OK, it's just pointing to good that can come out of bad. It's also important to say that if we can't see growth, it doesn't mean we're a bad person; we haven't failed. Often these things take many years, and it would be dangerous to suggest we gloss over the grief someone is experiencing and point to the positives that have come out of their experiences. We don't move from a state of trauma and grief to a state of growth – the two can happen simultaneously.

Growth also depends a number of factors. One that people point to is having relationships where they feel 'nurtured, liberated or validated' and when they know they are genuinely accepted by other people.[5] The ability to connect with people who do this for us and support us through active, attentive and compassionate listening can lead not only to recovery but can also foster post-traumatic growth. This may include a therapist, close friend, family member, spiritual leader and/or mentor.

Sheridan Voysey, in his beautiful book *The Making of Us*, discusses how when a trial meets a talent we often see growth. He says, 'So what if each crack in our hearts and every hole in our lives – from the loss of our health or status or power to our lack of a spouse or a child or a career – was the gap through which the divine grace waited to flow? What if our humbled status made us ready for the using, our sufferings poised to bring little resurrections? What if our empty spaces became channels for God's power.'[6]

The story of Joseph in the book of Genesis is a powerful reminder of this. He goes from being the favoured son to being sold into slavery by his jealous brothers and was taken to work for Potiphar. There he was promoted, and it looked like things were improving until Potiphar's wife took a shine to him and didn't take his rejection well. She had him thrown into prison where he remained for some time. Despite all of these awful, traumatic events, we are reminded that God was with Joseph (Gen. 39:2; 39:21). Eventually he was released from prison, having been able to give Pharaoh an interpretation to a dream that was troubling him. When he was later reunited with his brothers, he was able to say, 'You intended to harm me, but God intended it for good to accomplish what is now being done, the saving of many lives' (Gen. 50:20).

God was with Joseph throughout his trials. He took him from being a slave to being in the powerful position of being in charge of Pharaoh's palace. There, rather than delighting in wielding power, Joseph used his wisdom to save many from starvation during a severe famine.

God used Joseph where he was, in his place of suffering, but he was at work in Joseph's character too. We see Joseph go from being a spoilt and beloved son, who delighted in the idea of his brothers bowing down to him, to being a man who fully depended on God (Gen. 40:8; 41:16). He was able to extend grace and mercy to the brothers who had changed the course of his life. When Joseph chose a name for his second son, he decided on Ephraim, saying, 'It is because God has made me fruitful in the land of my suffering' (Gen. 41:52).

GRIT

Angela Duckworth is famous for developing research on grit; she wanted to see why some people succeeded in life and others didn't. She says:

> Grit isn't talent. Grit isn't luck. Grit isn't how intensely, for the moment, you want something. Instead, grit is about having what some researchers call an 'ultimate concern'—a goal you care about so much that it organizes and gives meaning to almost everything you do. And grit is holding steadfast to that goal. Even when you fall down. Even when you screw up. Even when progress toward that goal is halting or slow. Talent and luck matter to success. But talent and luck are no guarantee of grit. And in the very long run, I think grit may matter as least as much, if not more.'[7]

In Viktor Frankl's book, *Man's Search for Meaning*, which talks about his experiences of being a prisoner in a Nazi concentration camp, he describes a key moment in his survival. He was considering whether to trade his last cigarette for a bowl of soup and how to work with one of the sadistic foremen when he realised how meaningless his life had become. Of course, he couldn't escape or change his circumstances, but he realised what would help him survive was having purpose. He imagined himself giving a lecture once the war was finished, teaching on the psychology of the concentration camp to help others understand what it was like. He created concrete goals, even at a point when he didn't know if he would live, to help him keep going in the worst circumstances.[8] He said, 'He who has a why to live for can bear almost any how.'[9] When we have a purpose, we find the grit that keeps us going.

SPLASHES OF HEAVEN

One person who exemplifies grit, passion and perseverance is Joni Eareckson Tada. Joni was 17 when she broke her neck in a diving accident. On a day out with friends she dived into shallow water and severed her spinal cord. Until then, she had been healthy and athletic; suddenly her whole world changed. She became quadriplegic. She pleaded with God to heal her, repenting of any sin she could think of, getting prayer at any healing ministry she could find. Nothing changed. In the depths of depression, she didn't want to live. But she didn't have the physical ability to take pills or cut herself with a razor to find an escape, so she cried out to God, 'If I can't die, show me how to live.' She felt God wanted to do a far deeper healing in her than her physical healing: he wanted to heal her soul. The paralysed man mentioned in Chapter 5, who was healed by Jesus, was firstly healed from his sin (Mark 2:10–11). For Joni, that spoke into her heart as she accepted that her body would not be healed in this lifetime, but her soul would, and for her that was so much more important.

She began to reach out to others who are disabled and who faced similar challenges to her; those who were isolated and without hope. That was the start of the charity Joni and Friends, that still works across the globe 40 years later, offering practical assistance as well as providing Bibles and emotional and spiritual support. They want to see people with additional needs embracing Jesus, embracing life and embracing the circumstances they're in.[10] They help churches to embrace people of all abilities, and train and mentor people with disabilities to exercise leadership gifts within the church.

Despite the joy Joni finds in helping others, her life remains challenging. She needs at least seven helpers each week to help her do the things many of us take for granted, like washing, dressing and exercising, even brushing her teeth. Every day she wakes up and says, 'Jesus, I can't do this thing called life, please help me. Please show up; give me your strength because I can't make it through the day.' Because she's so dependent on God every moment of every day, she says she experiences the sweetest, most precious and most intimate relationship with him. It's now 46 years since her accident and Joni still lives with chronic pain. She recently had breast cancer and had to undergo chemotherapy. Driving home with her husband one day, they were talking about suffering being like splash overs of hell that wake us up from our spiritual slumber. They began to talk about what splash overs of heaven are; is it the times when everything is going well, we are healthy and everything is easy? No. Their conclusion after all they've been through is that 'splash overs of heaven are finding Jesus in your splash over of hell. To find Jesus in your hell is ecstasy beyond compare and I wouldn't trade it for any moment of walking in this world'.[11]

GOD'S GREAT STORY OF RESTORATION

Have you ever wondered what God's ultimate purpose is for this world he created? As a young child, I remember sitting in church hearing talks about the mysterious 'end times'. It felt like we were being told to hang on, check the fulfilment of prophecies off a wall-chart and wait to be raptured. As an adult, I came across two books which gave me a very different perspective: Tom Wright's *Surprised by Hope* and Tom Sine's *The Mustard Seed Conspiracy*. They explained that the point of Scripture wasn't that one day we are all going to escape up to heaven, but that God, through his loving kindness, was forming a new heaven and new earth now. Beautiful images of Isaiah 65 and John's vision in Revelation 21 show the new Jerusalem that comes down from heaven, where the earth is under

God's rule, and there is hope for the marginalised and those suffering from illness, depression, poverty and racial injustice.

We live in the tension of the 'now and not yet'; God's kingdom has come and is also coming. That's gives me hope for the future and real tangible hope for those of us who are suffering now. Writer and therapist K. J. Ramsey puts it like this, 'Hope in suffering is never for a disembodied day when we can finally escape the bodies, relationships and circumstances that have caused so much pain. Biblical hope is expressed not in certainty but in curiosity, hearts that acknowledge and accept Jesus is already King, lives that look for restoration of his rule right here, people propelled by a willingness to see Jesus turn every inch of creation from cursed to cured. The relationships that were broken made right; our relationship to our bodies, each other, the earth and God will be fully and finally restored.'[12]

The key for me was realising that God's ultimate purpose for human history is his purpose for me now. Hope becomes tangible in the here and now if you believe God is in the restoration business. As I understand more of the Bible, I see that hope springs up from the ruins, life comes from the wilderness. God works through the most awful circumstances.

Hope is very different from optimism; true hope comes from a deeper place. The parable of the mustard seed shows that the smallest seeds can grow to provide shade for the broken. Small acts of love and kindness, our actions in the here and now, do matter. Those actions that are born out of tragedy can make a difference to so many lives.

I wonder if we can allow God into every area of our lives, our past and current pain, just like Joni Eareckson Tada and Grace Idowu. Though that doesn't mean our pain will disappear, we choose to trust God with our story. As we look to find ourselves in his big story of redemption, we start to find meaning even in the difficult times.

I don't believe that God caused all the tragedies that I have seen and experienced, but I cannot deny that I have been changed by them in a way that I hope makes me more approachable, more loving and more understanding of others when they are struggling. I have sat in the dark with my own shame, feeling like I've failed and I'm beyond repair, and I don't want anyone else to feel that if I can help it. I feel more committed than ever to communicating and demonstrating the love of God through my life in order to help others flourish. I don't have all the answers anymore; my Christianity used to be quite black and white whereas now it is full of grey and mystery.

One change I can see is that I react differently to pressured situations. When my book *Honesty Over Silence* came out, my emails increased and the stories were so moving, but this time I wasn't floored by them in the same way as I had been in the past. I knew I couldn't take total responsibility for people. I have always wanted to do my best, but I can't look after everyone and everything. Instead, I want to guide people into the presence of Jesus, knowing he is the one who can help them.

Learning about resilience has helped me know I can feel the heat of the sun but not always be burned by it. Liggy Webb, a consultant in behavioural skills and author of *Resilience*, says 'the best thing anyone described [resilience] to me as, was "emotional sun-screen"; it's not covering yourself with a protective shield but it is about creating a protective layer'.[13]

When I talk about this, people often ask, 'Are you glad you went through all those challenges with your mental and physical health as God has used it so much to help others?' Honestly? I'm not there yet. I still have sleepless nights; I still sometimes feel isolated because of my mental health challenges. The memories of the physical pain are too fresh for me to wipe them away and say I'm glad for them. I wouldn't wish what I went through on anyone. But I'm on the journey and I am thankful for what God has brought out of my pain. Kintsugi Hope wouldn't exist without it. In a strange way, my pain has opened doors like this book for me to tell people like you how much God loves you and how crazy he is about you. The pain hasn't been wasted.

CHAPTER 7

WHAT IS SUCCESS?

My subconscious view of success – of a good life – for many years was that I needed to be the rescuer and take responsibility for everyone and everything. I don't think I'm alone in that. It can be particularly strong in Christian circles that we feel the need to fix *everything*. We want to keep everyone happy all the time but it's just not possible. We wind up exhausted and frustrated simply because we can't be perfect, and we don't have the capacity to make everything in the world better.

My daughter, Abigail, has taught me a lot about success. She is a beautiful soul who struggles with a condition called nystagmus. That means she only has about 40% vision and her eyes make repetitive, uncontrolled movements. As well as affecting vision, these movements often result in reduced depth perception and can affect balance and coordination. Her involuntary eye movements can occur from side to side, up and down, or in a circular pattern; rarely do we have a family mealtime when she doesn't knock over a drink by accident. As Abi has got older she gets more frustrated at not being able to see as well as everyone else. This has been combined with many years of trying to work out what additional needs she has. Endless hospital appointments could only conclude that she has special complex needs.

Abi never comes top of her class. She never gets the part she wants in the school assembly. She can't even get the 100% attendance certificate because she misses so much school due to hospital appointments. But... she regularly displays the kind of kindness and empathy you don't often see in adults, let alone in children her own age. When her school report comes home, she gets an A for effort in the majority of her subjects. She has the most generous heart and she makes me want to be a better person. Though at times she can get very frustrated at me, she makes my heart sing. I love her just the way she is and I don't want her to be anything else other than who she is: my Abigail. I worry for her when I see the pressure many put on young people to achieve academically, but then I remember what I look for when I employ someone: kindness, integrity, compassion and the ability to work well in a team are all high on my list. Not every achievement can be graded or quantified.

We live in a culture that promotes perfection as success. We need the perfect life, the perfect job, the perfect body, the perfect home, the perfect relationship. (And we need to show each of them off on Instagram at every opportunity, creating the perfect social media account.) Our cultural norms need challenging because they are doing nothing to help us, as evidenced by the growing mental health crisis. God never promised us perfection, in fact, he told us this life would have trouble (John 16:33). He also never expected us to be perfect.

One verse that has caused people to think he does is Matthew 5:48, which says, 'Be perfect, therefore, as your heavenly Father is perfect.' One guy told me that this verse was the reason he couldn't stand Christians, 'They're always trying to be perfect and think they're better than others but they never achieve it.' As a stand-alone verse, this has such power to worry us, especially any of us prone to perfectionism.

To put it back in to context, Jesus said this during the Sermon on the Mount, his manifesto for living with kingdom values, urging us to value the things that are truly worth valuing. The Greek word translated 'perfect' is *teleios*, which means moving towards completion and wholeness. Ledger and Bray compare this to the work of an artist bringing their painting to completion, stroke by stroke; it's not perfect but it's on its way. They say, 'That's how God sees us: a work in progress, going on towards completion when perfection will be seen.'[1]

New Testament theologian Paula Gooder says, 'The Greek word here is *teleios* and it can mean "perfect" but is more usually used to refer to maturity or wholeness.' She points out that it's the same word used in 1 Corinthians 2:6, 'Yet among the *mature* we do speak wisdom'; Philippians 3:15, 'Let those of us then who are *mature* be of the same mind'; and James 1:4, 'Let endurance have its full effect, so that you may be *mature* and complete' (NRSV, italics mine). Gooder concludes, 'So, a possible alternative translation would be "Be mature as your Father in heaven is mature". The trouble is that's no better – it just doesn't sound right though it is probably closer to what Jesus meant. Be rounded, be whole, be complete as God is. God does not say one thing and think another; God does not pretend compassion while really not caring at all. God is sincere, whole and wholehearted, and we should be too. That is how we reveal that we are deeply and richly rooted in God's commands.'

It is also important to note that the tense of verb used in the verse is the future tense, meaning that one precious day we will be made perfect in Jesus.

God is not asking for perfection. He is looking at our hearts, our motives, our desires. 'The Lord does not look at the things people look at. People look at the outward appearance, but the Lord looks at the heart' (1 Sam. 16:7).

PERFECTIONISM

I always believed that perfectionism affected those kids whose parents put too much pressure on them to perform at school. My parents never did that so I figured it wasn't an issue I needed to deal with. Yet a few years ago, as I was studying for a talk, I suddenly realised how I had misunderstood perfectionism. I now realise it is on a continuum and I can move up and down on that continuum at different times.

Brené Brown says, 'Perfectionism is not self-improvement. Perfectionism is, at its core, about trying to earn approval. Most perfectionists grew up being praised for achievement and performance (grades, manners, rule following, people pleasing, appearance, sports). Somewhere along the way, they adopted this dangerous and debilitating belief system: "I am what I accomplish and how well I accomplish it. Please. Perform. Perfect." Healthy striving is self-focused: How can I improve? Perfectionism is other-focused: What will they think? Perfectionism is a hustle.'[2]

It wasn't until I understood how perfectionism revealed itself in my life that I truly understood its power and how it related to a lack of resilience. Everyone has a different idea of what perfect is, so it's like trying to hit a moving target. You please one set of people and realise another set think you've done the wrong thing. You achieve perfection in one person's eyes but someone else has a different definition. Trying to be perfect really affected my ability to bounce forwards; I kept getting stuck. To become resilient, to thrive in adversity, I need to have a better definition of success.

As I studied and researched the characteristics of perfectionism I started to see its prevalence in my life. I wonder if you can recognise any of your own thought patterns in these descriptions of mine?

- **Catastrophic thinking.** The smallest argument with Diane is the end of our marriage. The kids get angry with me and I am the worst dad in the world. A small disagreement at work can play on loop in my head until I have blown it up out of all proportion. I will confront my colleague and then realise they can't even remember the conversation that has been torturing me and certainly weren't harbouring any bad feeling about it.

- **Mind reading.** This is linked to catastrophic thinking. I think I know what others think of me. It's based on very little evidence and it is rarely positive.

- **Unrealistic expectations.** During lockdown my most common thoughts were, 'I am a failure' and 'I am a terrible parent'. If it was a friend who had four kids at home and a full-time job, I would say, 'Go easy on yourself', but for me, I felt like I should be doing better. I struggled to understand the kids' schoolwork, I struggled to teach two of them at a time and run Kintsugi Hope, but instead of cutting myself some slack, I told myself I was a failure.

- **Rigid belief system.** I use words like 'I should, I must, I ought', which mean constantly feeling like I'm not measuring up. There is very little flexibility in my thinking and if I miss my self-imposed deadlines I feel bad.

- **Hate making mistakes.** Living with such high standards means you are going to make mistakes, it's inevitable. Yet rather than seeing them as a necessary step towards achievement, the mistakes eat away at me, leaving me frustrated.

- **Overcompensating.** I work so hard in order to get everything right, overcompensating in my behaviour and pushing myself to the limit.

- **Excessive checking.** I don't want to make mistakes or let people down or offend anyone. I want my friendships to be perfect, so I will double check emails and texts. At work, I constantly look for reassurance my ideas aren't rubbish.

- **Decision making.** I don't want to get a decision wrong so I procrastinate. Even small decisions are hard. (After half an hour of flicking through all the options on Netflix, my family often shout at me, 'JUST CHOOSE A FILM – ANY FILM! WE DON'T CARE ANYMORE!')

- **Receiving feedback.** Perfectionists find feedback very hard to hear, whether it's positive or negative. Diane is my biggest fan and my biggest critic and she always tries to remind me that just because there is feedback, it doesn't always make it true. If I hear ten positive comments and one negative, I focus in on the one. For perfectionists, that means we fail to celebrate achievements.

- **People-pleasing.** When we're trying to have perfect relationships, we will try to avoid saying anything that will rock the boat. I hate upsetting people, so before talking to them about something tricky, I will rehearse the conversation in my head. I can also take it too personally when someone challenges me, even though I know that disagreement can be a healthy and important part of any relationship. When we become too focused on pleasing others, we start to act differently around people, which means we don't allow them to see our authentic self.

In Christian culture, it can sometimes be harder to spot perfectionism and approval seeking as it can easily be hidden behind activity. Communicator and author Sheila Walsh says, 'If you show up drunk at your Bible study, people will notice. If your weight has skyrocketed, it shows up in the real world. But if you're the one who volunteers for everything at church, who leads a Bible study, who speaks, who sits on national television every day and talks about the love of God, only he knows whether you're serving out of pain or passion, out of genuine calling or a devastating wound.'[3]

Often the values we are living by are actually setting ourselves up for failure. If one of our main aims is to be liked and accepted by everyone, the chances of us failing are 100%. It is impossible to please everyone all the time. There is only one man who has lived a perfect life and he didn't keep everyone happy. People got angry with him all the time, to the point that they crucified him. Ledger and Bray say in *Insight into Perfectionism*, 'High expectations and clear goals are not bad in themselves: they help us do – and be – the best we can. But when they are rigid and concrete they can cause stress and anxiety. Perfectionism can undoubtedly have a positive effect, in helping others to aim high and in paying attention to necessary detail. But if we continually strive to be perfect to such an extent that we feel a failure when we're not, we will always feel we fall short.'[4]

This reminds me of the fact that when hunters want to trap a monkey, they take a coconut and make a hole in it, put some food inside it and then tie the coconut to a tree. The monkey comes along, reaches inside and grabs the food. But with its hand in a fist it can't get it back out of the coconut. It has a choice: let go of the food and be free, or hold on to it and be trapped. As this is an effective monkey trap there are no prizes for guessing which it does. Stupid monkey. We would never be that dumb. Would we? Would we hold on to things that look like something we want but are actually trapping us and causing us pain? I'm still in the process of learning to let go of what other people think of me, because that causes me huge anxiety. I have to let go of my ego, where I'm trying to impress other people. I have to let go of my inner critic; he doesn't serve me well and I have to instead trust the Holy Spirit to convict me as he needs to without me speaking guilt and blame over myself.

Psalm 46:10 is often translated as 'Be still, and know that I am God.' Shelia Walsh comments, 'The original Hebrew root of "be still" doesn't mean "be quiet"; it means "let go". That's very different, don't you think? Let go and know that I am God! Let go of trying to control your spouse! Let go of your worry about your finances! Let go of your unforgiveness! Let go of your past! Let go of what you can't control—and rest in the knowledge that God is in control!'[5]

LIVING BY OUR VALUES

I love this quote from William Carey: 'I am not scared of failure; I am scared of succeeding at things that don't matter.'

We can't have the 'perfect' life but we can live by our values. We can't choose how life turns out but we can choose how we respond to it. Living by our values is more important that being perfect; it can lead us to contentment regardless of our circumstances.

After surviving the Holocaust, Viktor Frankl wrote, 'We who lived in concentration camps can remember the men who walked through the huts comforting others, giving away their last piece of bread. They may have been in few in number, but they offered sufficient proof that everything can be taken from a man but one thing: the last of human freedoms – to choose one's attitude in any given set of circumstances, to choose one's own way.'[6]

We think of success as what we do. But it's not just what you do, it's how you do it that is so important. What are you for? Values give you a strong foundation to make key decisions from. I always think of values as roots of trees. I want my values to go so deep that, whatever the storms of life, I know they won't change. Others refer to values as rocks you can cling to on a stormy sea, keeping your feet fixed on the ground. Values are the cornerstones to our lives. Values are chosen and active, they help choose the way you want to live your life; they are a way to keep asking the questions 'what matters the most to me?' and 'what do I want to invest my time in to and who with?' Author Susan David says, 'Your core values provide a compass that keeps you moving in the right direction.'[7] I love the idea of values being like a compass, helping us know the direction of travel even if we are not always sure of the destination.

If you want to achieve success, you need to know the metrics you are measuring success against. If one of your values is living in community but, due to the demands of a busy job say, you don't have any close connections locally, you're not living out of your values. Though that busy job may afford you a big house, great car, fabulous holidays and all the other things many people call 'success', the reality is you will probably feel like a failure because of your own barometer as to what's important. I found this a helpful way of looking at values, that they '[should] determine your priorities, and, deep down, they're probably the measures you use to tell if your life is turning out the way you want it to. When the things that you do and the way you behave match your values, life is usually good – you're satisfied and content. But when these don't align with your personal values, that's when things feel... wrong. This can be a real source of unhappiness.'[8]

Author Mark Manson points out the difference between good and bad values, saying, 'Healthy values are achieved internally. Something like creativity and humility can be experienced right now. You simply have to orient your mind in a certain way to experience it. These values are immediate and controllable and engage you with the world as it is rather than how you wish it were. Bad values are generally reliant on external events. Bad values, while sometimes fun or pleasurable, lie outside of your control and often require socially destructive or superstitious means to achieve.'[9]

One of my key values is relationship. I love to work with people I know and I work better in a small team. When I started XLP, I knew everyone extremely well and we were a close-knit bunch. As the work we did expanded and the team grew, it was impossible to be close with 70 people, and I found this really difficult. Over the years, occasionally a headhunter would ring me and ask if I would consider taking another job with a bigger staff team and bigger salary. Hear me right: neither of those things are bad. It's just that for me, I know I come alive in small teams, and so I made decisions about work based on my value of relationship.

Defining good and bad values can be challenging but vitally important if you want to be content. There are so many different measures of success, so many things people and culture will try to tell you is the path to contentment, but success is following your heart and doing what God is calling you to do and being who he is calling you to be.

As Susan David says, 'By knowing who you are and what you stand for, you come to life's choices with the most powerful tool of all: your full self.'[10]

COUNTERCULTURAL VALUES

For me, my purpose and my values don't simply come from my life experiences or my family upbringing, they come from my pursuit of my understanding of God. I believe the words of Jesus when he said the most important things we can ever do are to love God with all our heart, mind and strength and to love our neighbour as ourselves (Mark 12:30–31). As a Christian, I want to align myself with Christ's values, which are often countercultural: he says the weak are strong; the humble, the meek and the marginalised should be prioritised. He values love, humility, sacrifice, honesty, mercy, justice, grace and community, all worked out in the messiness of life.

Culture values productivity but Jesus calls us to rest in him, and God commanded his people to have a Sabbath day of rest. Society tells us we should value financial security – Jesus tells us to trust everything to God. Again, the Bible isn't saying that productivity or financial security are wrong, just that we should look to God for our purpose and value.

A number of years ago, I was asked to speak in the main meeting at a large Christian festival. There were about 10,000 people in the meeting and I was pretty nervous. It felt like a real honour and I wanted to do a good job for those who had worked so hard to make the event what it was. A few hours before, I was told the talk was also going to be broadcast live on TV. It made me gulp a bit but there was only one opinion that really mattered to me that night. My daughter, Keziah, was attending the festival with her youth group. I stood on the stage, bright lights in my eyes, and kept scanning the crowd looking for her face. I tuned out the crowd and the thought of people watching on TV and kept thinking, 'Oh man, I hope Kez is liking this.' At the end of the talk, I stood by the side of the stage and there was a queue of people who wanted to chat about my talk and what God was saying to them. Each one deserved my attention but I just couldn't wait until I could speak to my daughter. All I cared about that night was what she thought. (Her conclusion was, thankfully, 'It wasn't rubbish', which is music to her dad's ears.) I long to live like that in my relationship with God, tuning out the crowd and focusing on his voice alone. I want him to be the person I long to please above all else, and I know he views success very differently to the way the world does.

PAUL IN LOCKDOWN

Towards the end of Paul's life, he was in a kind of lockdown. He had been arrested many times and held in prison for years in Jerusalem and Caesarea, but because he was a Roman citizen, he was taken to Rome for his case to be heard. Though he wasn't imprisoned there, he also wasn't allowed to move around freely. For two years he lived in a rented house where soldiers would have been at the door to stop him leaving. Although he couldn't go out, he was able to welcome others in: 'For two whole years Paul stayed here in his own rented house and welcomed all who came to see him. He proclaimed the kingdom of God and taught about the Lord Jesus Christ – with all boldness and without hindrance!' (Acts 28:30–31)

I wonder what must have gone through Paul's mind. Was he frustrated at his restrictions? He had spent so much time travelling from place to place preaching the gospel and seeing all sorts of signs and wonders. Did he see this time at home as wasted? He could receive visitors and could teach about the kingdom but not in any great numbers. This might have felt like a time of despair, a failure; Paul, the greatest apostle to the Gentiles, locked in captivity. Yet from that place of captivity he wrote what are known as the prison letters (Ephesians, Philippians, Colossians and Philemon) which include these words:

> I'm glad in God, far happier than you would ever guess—happy that you're again showing such strong concern for me. Not that you ever quit praying and thinking about me. You just had no chance to show it. Actually, I don't have a sense of needing anything personally. I've learned by now to be quite content whatever my circumstances. I'm just as happy with little as with much, with much as with little. I've found the recipe for being happy whether full or hungry, hands full or hands empty. Whatever I have, wherever I am, I can make it through anything in the One who makes me who I am. (Phil. 4:10–13, *The Message*)

Paul wasn't born content. He had learned contentment through his amazing journey. He learned to see himself as 'the least of all the Lord's people' and to discover 'the boundless riches of Christ' (Eph. 3:8). Paul found contentment in his Saviour. He had learned to rejoice in God always, no matter what was going on around him (Phil. 4:4).

I love this prayer from Thomas Merton, an American Trappist monk.

> My Lord God,
> I have no idea where I am going.
> I do not see the road ahead of me.
> I cannot know for certain where it will end
> nor do I really know myself,
> and the fact that I think I am following your will
> does not mean that I am actually doing so.
> But I believe that the desire to please you
> does in fact please you.
> And I hope I have that desire in all that I am doing.
> I hope that I will never do anything apart from that desire.
> And I know that if I do this you will lead me by the right road,
> though I may know nothing about it.
> Therefore will I trust you always though
> I may seem to be lost and in the shadow of death.
> I will not fear, for you are ever with me,
> and you will never leave me to face my perils alone.

This prayer sums it up for me: my job is to make sure my heart is right before God. He rejoices in the best we can do; God doesn't want perfection, he wants us to do our best. Success isn't the amount of work I can get done in a day, the amount of likes that I get on social media or the amount of money in the bank. It can't always be measured by external things. For me it is knowing I have nothing to prove in order to make me loveable to God as his love never changes. Success is looking in the mirror and not wanting to change what I see, knowing that God loves me for me. It's knowing that he wants me to show up, to my thoughts, my feelings, my doubts. It's being present to my family, friends and colleagues. It's being authentically known.

As a child, I used to love mystery and uncertainty, but as I got older the need to be in control became key. I no longer find uncertainty exciting; I find it terrifying. Bouncing forwards means finding ways to be comfortable with uncertainty and mystery; finding the humility and courage to know we can't control everything. Resilience and bouncing forwards aren't about finding the perfect life, because life does not need to be perfect for us to find contentment in the here and now.

LIZ'S STORY

I first came across Liz Carter by reading her book *Catching Contentment*, which powerfully combines theological insight with her own story.[1] I was really pleased to endorse her second book, *Treasure in Dark Places: Stories and Poems of Hope in the Hurting*, which is a collection of beautiful poems. I have interviewed Liz for my TV show on TBN, and she always comes across as so genuine and authentic. She inspires me to keep going when I feel life is tough and to hang onto God without having to resort to platitudes. Liz models dignity no matter what she's dealing with.

I was a sickly child and many of my earliest memories are of lying in bed shivering, countless trips to the doctors and being in and out of hospital. I had repeated chest infections, pneumonia and bronchitis; the only thing medical professionals could tell my parents was that I had a weak chest, possibly asthma, but they couldn't give me a proper diagnosis. As I grew older it became more apparent that I was different from the other kids. They would run round the PE track while I struggled far behind, frustration radiating from teachers who thought I just wasn't trying hard enough. The other kids laughed at me and I knew I was different. I just couldn't do what they could do and I didn't know why. It was hard to make friends as I spent so much time off school and by the time I was a teenager I was being bullied quite badly. Even the teachers were fed up with me and as I sat shivering in classes, the aches of my body written all over my face; they would sigh, 'Ill again?' I felt like I wasn't enough.

I lost great chunks of my education being off for weeks and weeks at a time and there was no way of making up what I'd missed. Back then, there was no support for children like me, we were just expected to catch up when we were well which, of course, was impossible with the amount of time I was absent. My teachers continued to misunderstand me and my reports from those years say that I wasn't trying hard enough when actually I was doing all that I could given the circumstances. I had a passion for English from a young age and loved to read and write, but even my English teachers thought I wasn't doing well enough and I grew discouraged.

Somehow I passed a few GCSEs and went on to do A levels, determined that I wanted to be a teacher so I could help children learn to read and write. I tried to convince myself that it would be fine, that I would be well enough to teach but, although I passed my degree, each time I was ill and couldn't make it in to teach my class I felt awful. I didn't want to let the children down and I knew it was hard for the school to keep covering for me. Again I felt like the odd one out. So many teachers battled through colds and other illnesses in order to be there for their class, whereas I was regularly laid up in bed with no choice but to stay home for weeks at a time. I felt like I was letting them down and that they all looked at me as though I wasn't up to being a teacher. It's hard to shake the feeling that people think you are weak or lazy, especially when you have no medical diagnosis to explain why you're ill so severely and so regularly.

In the meantime, I met my husband Tim. We got married and a few years later decided to start a family. But during my pregnancy I got pneumonia. I was so unwell that the doctors said I couldn't go back to work, so I had to start claiming benefits. At that time it was called Invalidity Benefit and that's how I felt: invalid.

When our daughter arrived, I sank everything into motherhood. My passion and purpose as a teacher had been taken away from me by illness and I was desperate for a new sense of identity. Of course, the illnesses didn't stop and I couldn't be the wonder mum I'd dreamt of being. We had another child, a son this time, and I found myself stuck in the house, unwell, and feeling like I was failing my children. Tim was working long hours so I was their main carer and yet I was exhausted and in pain most days. I got postnatal depression, and felt like I wasn't enough for my children. I would look on social media and see families on fun days out and holidays. They were doing normal things but they just seemed so far outside my reach with the little energy that I had. I worried I was letting my kids down and that they weren't having the childhood they deserved.

Throughout all of this I had prayed many times that God would heal me. The teaching I was hearing told me that God was willing and able to heal me, so if I wasn't better the problem must lie with me. 'You've not got enough faith' I was told. 'There must be sin in your life,' said others. 'Just thank God by faith that you are healed and whole and you will be' wasn't uncommon. I was given Bible verses to 'claim' by reciting them three times a day like a charm. One hospital chaplaincy volunteer came to my bedside and said that Jesus healed people so if I wasn't healed I was calling Jesus a liar. Although that made me feel terrible, thankfully I knew it wasn't true. I was able to hold on to the truth that God was with me in the darkness. He wasn't cross with me that I wasn't healed. He wasn't blaming me for my lack of faith. He wasn't saying that I wasn't good enough or that I wasn't working hard enough. I knew enough to know that's not how he works.

In fact, one of my most profound encounters with God happened when I was ten years old and in the middle of a horrible infection. I'd gone to a Christian camp with my family and our church and, having given my life to Jesus just a few years before, I was excited to learn more about God. I went to my group one night and could feel the familiar shivers starting alongside the creeping pain that told me I was about to get wiped out with an infection. I was still desperate to go to the meeting so one of my friends suggested I ask a leader to pray for me. They told me God would heal me if I asked him and I believed them. Thankfully the leader was a gentle and wise young man who didn't make any rash promises about God healing me, instead he prayed that I would encounter God.

A peace came over me like nothing I'd known. Then what felt like a shot of electricity went through my body. I began speaking in tongues, which was something I'd heard about but had never experienced before. God didn't heal me but I still remember almost running back to our caravan that night with an indescribable joy. I was still in pain and exhausted from the growing fever and had to lie down and go to sleep, but God had met with me in a beautiful way. What I didn't know then was that this encounter would encapsulate what God would do in my life for many years to come. He wasn't going to heal the illness, not to date anyway, but he was going to meet me in it.

I've had a mixed relationship with receiving prayer ever since, especially since I was diagnosed in my thirties with bronchiectasis. It's such a rare lung condition that doctors hadn't thought to look for it, and it was only after a CT scan that the extent of what was going on was revealed. Finally, I was given a term that helped me understand I had more than just 'weak lungs'. While this meant I could be put on continuous antibiotics and receive other treatments, there is no cure. This new label sometimes felt like it was a target on my back saying I was 'the sick one'. People wanted to pray and see me healed, which was a blessing in many ways, but sometimes it felt like that healing was less about me and more about them. It can be incredibly damaging when someone assumes what you want prayer for because they've labelled you as sick.

They'd jump right in, praying aggressively and proclaiming healing before getting in my face and saying, 'WELL?' This was obviously my cue to say I had been healed and all was well. Each time I've had to reply that I'm still in pain and watch the person's face fall in disappointment. Sometimes they would rally and say, 'We need to keep praying and pressing on,' without asking me how I felt about that, and their prayers would get louder and more aggressive while I waited uncomfortably for them to finish. Other times they would shrug their shoulders, lose interest and walk away. It's hard not to feel you are disappointing people by still being sick; a clearly unwelcome burden to add to those you're already carrying. The majority of people are more careful and when someone prays for you sensitively it can be such a balm to your weary body and soul. At the New Wine conference one year, a woman I'd never met came over and said she'd felt God nudge her to pray for me. She quietly prayed for God's presence and it was just what I needed. Having people pray for healing that doesn't come can be vulnerable and absolutely exhausting but I would always welcome prayers for God's presence. I loved that she didn't have an agenda and I always appreciate it when people don't assume what I want prayer for, even when they know I have a lung disease.

Of course, there has been a huge amount of disappointment to process in the fact that I haven't been healed. Many hours as I was overcome with pain I would ask, 'What am I doing wrong? Why is my faith not enough?' I'd be at large conferences and watch people stream to the stage to share their stories of miraculous healing. My heart would be a mix of joy for them and the freedom they were now experiencing as well as discontent and a little voice saying, 'Why not me? God, why haven't you healed me? Have you forgotten me?'

That pain and disappointment led me to really study God's Word for myself. I knew that Jesus healed people, I knew that God was powerful, but I wanted to see what else the Bible had to say to someone like me. The more I looked, the more I realised that the Bible was full of weak and broken people. Not just sinners but people who were sick, disabled and in pain. I saw people like Paul who set a great example of faith despite the hardship and persecution he faced. I saw that while Jesus healed people, he also *saw* them. He asked people what they wanted; he didn't put words in their mouth or pray for their healing without their permission. I learnt that his heart was for people in pain. He didn't use people to show his power, he loved people and wanted them to have fullness of life. Slowly I began to see that fullness of life isn't about being whole physically.

Paul's words particularly caught my attention: 'I know what it is to be in need, and I know what it is to have plenty. I have learned the secret of being content in any and every situation, whether well fed or hungry, whether living in plenty or in want. I can do all this through him who gives me strength' (Phil. 4:12–13).

A thought began to take root: could I find contentment without being healed? Each day I experience pain and exhaustion. Even on a 'good' day I will still need to rest or sleep at some point to be able to carry on. Bronchiectasis means mucus pools at the bottom of my lungs and when it gets infected (which is regularly) it's incredibly painful. As I breathe, the pain shoots up my side and into my shoulder, reverberating around my back as though I'm being stabbed with knives. I catch pneumonia a lot and often it's in both lungs (double pneumonia) which needs two weeks of IV antibiotics to shift. Around once a year I am back in hospital because I require more medication and care than I can be given at home.

Given all this, what would contentment look like for me? The culture of our day tells us that contentment comes when we have the best of everything, and the perspective that has snuck into Christianity is that God simply wants our happiness, but I wasn't convinced by either of these, so I started to ask God to show me more about true contentment.

Asking that question led me on a significant journey of emotional and spiritual healing as God showed me so much about his character and his heart. I realised I needed to look to Jesus in everything and invest in my relationship with God above anything else. Even when I'm ill and can't pick up my Bible, I can still keep my mind on what is holy, good, righteous and true (Phil. 4:8). For me, that's been a huge part of learning resilience in my struggles. I have to surrender to God, and to know that he's got me. I don't believe for a minute that God has caused me to have this illness or that this was his great design for my life. But I've also had to come to a place of peace where I don't live waiting for healing or in despair about my circumstances. I choose to be grateful that God is working in me in spite of *and* because of *and* within my situation.

One woman who inspired me to see that contentment can be found in any circumstance was Hae Woo, a Christian who spent many years in a labour camp in North Korea for her faith. She tells how God worked in her life right there in that dark pit of a place and it helped changed my perspective of God giving us easy lives when we choose to follow him. I saw how high her faith levels were – she risked her life by meeting with others to worship, even in a toilet as that was the only place they could gather without a guard watching them. The Bible is full of people who suffered tremendous hardship as they've followed God, and God never makes us any promises about life being easy.

Learning all of this was a radical shift in perspective for me, but that's not to say it's been plain sailing ever since. I've certainly had my moments when I've cried out, 'Are you there, God? Are you truly good?' One particularly bad time was when I was in hospital with yet another bout of pneumonia. The pain was so all-consuming I remember very little about it except crying out that I was in more agony than when I gave birth.

Tim sat beside my bed, unable to do anything to ease my suffering, and I remember his anger, questioning why a loving, caring God would leave me to such pain. We had no peace, just so many questions. There was no lightning bolt moment that day, no answer from heaven to reassure us of God's presence. But as we sat in that pit, feeling like we'd hit rock bottom, we began the gradual process of knowing God was with us. He was still there even when we couldn't see him or feel him. We chose the words of the psalmists as our praise and comfort to say, 'Yet I will still praise him'. We chose to say 'You are good' even though in that moment it didn't feel like he was good. We knew God's grace and that he understood our fragile human nature. We were reassured by the writings of Scripture that showed us others who had been in pain and had known it was OK to call out to God and question him. Psalms, Job and Lamentations are examples of writings that show God is big enough to handle our pain and our questions. We took comfort from that.

We felt God's encouragement to take off our masks, to put away any sense of a pretend, shiny gospel that says everything is fine. We held on to the truth that it is OK not to be OK. Fake faith brings no peace or contentment, but faith that wrestles with God in the darkness brings sustenance to our souls in the hard times. We can be raw with God and with one another and lay bare our feelings. We don't have to hold anything back but we can choose to praise God even in the midst of our questions.

We have learnt to be vulnerable with others too, sharing our pain, our questions, our disappointment, and are grateful for those who haven't tried to cover everything over with a pat answer. I've realised there's no point in pretending I'm OK and then walking away quietly breaking; I need to admit my vulnerability and lean on other people, asking for their prayers and accepting their help when needed. People want to help and it can be a lifeline when someone cooks us a meal when I've been particularly unwell, but it feels vulnerable to say yes even so. I've seen that the more vulnerable I am the more it fosters vulnerability in those around me. We no longer all hide away, trying to cover our pain, but we support one another, recognising we are all in need at different times; that's part of what it means to be human.

I've learnt that as well as accepting the kindness of others, it's key to my resilience to be kind to myself when I'm in pain. For many years I beat myself up for not being more productive, hearing those voices from my childhood telling me I was weak and lazy. Being so unkind to yourself just shatters you, it does nothing to help you heal. Now I know that sometimes I have to lie down or sit and watch Netflix; that's what resilience looks like for me some days.

God has made me more whole as he's worked so much in my emotions and spirit. I know that even when I've got nothing left, I can call out to him and he'll be there. I'm more aware than ever that I need his presence and love so much more than I need his physical healing. Ultimately we're all human and will all die; my goal in prayer isn't to convince God to heal me physically but to ask him to show me his nearness and presence in my life.

I've had to learn that when I'm struggling with pain and infections, God doesn't expect me to have an amazing prayer life. I have to let go of the desire to strive to earn his love and attention, and not take on guilt of not studying my Bible every day when I'm in pain and too weak to hold a book let alone get out of bed. He hears the cries of my heart when I feel at the end of myself and all I can say is 'I need you'.

I've found watching worship videos has been healing and allows me to soak in God's presence when I can do nothing but lie still. I know now that God will meet me where I am. We can think it's on us to 'find' him, but he's here with us already and we don't have to do anything to please him.

Some people have said that God has given me this disease in order to use me to help other people. I know their hearts are good and they mean to encourage me by saying that God can use the difficulties I've faced to bless other people in their journeys. What I've realised is that I don't want to hear God is using me – I want to hear that he loves me. That's what's important. I'm not a tool he picks up and puts down, I'm a child that he loves, and he loves me whether I'm having a good day or a bad day. I'm grateful beyond measure that I can do things that help other people; I know what it's like to feel lonely in your pain and like you're the only one, and I want to do all I can to reach others in their darkness and shine some of God's light and life there. But I believe God wants to partner with me rather than use me.

As I look back, I honestly don't think I could have had a better life than the one I've lived. It might sound strange and I don't say it glibly, but I feel like I've been on an adventure with God. I've journeyed with him through the ups and downs and I've realised life isn't about having everything you ever dreamed of and great mountaintop experiences, it's about meeting with God in the everyday highs and lows. There have been many hard things but I've also known God close and have learnt that he loves me and that we can find contentment in him no matter what our circumstances.

CHAPTER 8

KINDNESS IS THE BEST DRUG

Kindness gets confused with being nice, passive or weak, when actually it's a skill that involves courage and vulnerability. True kindness involves reaching out to others and remembering we need to be kind to ourselves too. I believe people are intrinsically good, that there is a desire in all of us to love and be kind. An article in *Psychologies* magazine said, 'You've heard about survival of the fittest and Darwin. Survival of the fittest is usually associated with selfishness, meaning that to survive [a basic instinct] means to look out for yourself. But Darwin, who studied human evolution, actually didn't see mankind as being biologically competitive and self-interested. Darwin believed that we are a profoundly social and caring species. He argued that sympathy and caring for others is instinctual.'[1]

In Christian teaching there is often talk of original sin, meaning we all have a fallen nature, but I also believe in original goodness. Six times during creation God evaluated what he had created as being good (Gen. 1:4,10,12,18,21,25), and it culminated in the finished creation being declared 'very good' (1:31). 'Original goodness' was a phrase used by Eknath Easwaran in his book of the same title to signify the spark of divinity hidden in every one of us that gives us the spiritual resources of love, compassion, meaning, hope and freedom from fear. There is a sense that to be fully human means we need to connect with each other through love and kindness.

Anne Frank, who wrote a diary during the German occupation of Holland during the Second World War, saw the worst of human nature up close and said, 'In spite of everything, I still believe that people are really good at heart.'[2] Author Roald Dahl said, 'I think probably kindness is my number one attribute in a human being. I'll put it before any of the things like courage or bravery or generosity or anything else... Kindness – that simple word. To be kind – covers everything to my mind. If you're kind that's it.'[3]

If it all sounds a bit wishy-washy, there is scientific evidence to show the benefits kindness has on our brains and our bodies. Being kind releases oxytocin, dopamine and serotonin – all known as 'happy hormones', which explains why studies have shown that kindness can be a successful treatment for pain, depression and anxiety. Only God could design a system where doing something for others actually helps you at the same time!

Take volunteering. Author Christine Carter says, 'People who volunteer tend to experience fewer aches and pains.

Giving help to others protects overall health twice as much as aspirin protects against heart disease. People 55 and older who volunteer for two or more organizations have an impressive 44% lower likelihood of dying early, and that's after sitting out every other contributing factor, including physical health, exercise, gender, habits like smoking, marital status and many more. This is a stronger effect than exercising four times a week or going to church.[4]

Jesus showed us how love, kindness and compassion go hand in hand. I'm always so challenged by his example, especially how he made time for people. He didn't mind being interrupted or inconvenienced, whether it was by a group of friends digging a hole in his roof, a woman who was bleeding who reached out to touch his cloak, or a blind man shouting at him from the side of the road. I hate being interrupted and, if I'm not careful, I know that people around me can end up feeling they are less important than my work. Because I place a high value on relationships, I have to continually challenge myself to remember that love takes time. You can't rush walking beside people.

Jesus operated from a place of compassion.[5] Kindness and compassion are very subtly different but deeply entwined, and both are vital for resilience. Kindness can focus more on outward actions, whereas compassion is a deep feeling. Often feeling compassion for someone can lead to an act of kindness.

One of my favourite Bible stories is where Jesus is walking along the road to Emmaus, which we read in Luke 24. He meets two travellers who were making the seven-mile journey from Jerusalem to Emmaus. It probably took about three hours to walk. As the two travellers went, they discussed the crucifixion of Jesus just days earlier and the reports of his resurrection. Most theologians believe the people to be Clopas and his wife, Mary, who many believe was there at the crucifixion alongside Mary the mother of Jesus and Mary Magdalene (John 19:25). If that is the case, Mary would have heard the cries from the cross and seen the spear that went into Jesus' side. She would have felt the agony, and the humiliation, of the crucifixion.

No wonder the couple were confused and heartbroken. In many ways, they were very ordinary people, without much influence in their culture. It's amazing to me that one of the first things Jesus did after his resurrection was to spend the morning walking alongside two heartbroken friends, allowing them space to talk. A marketing expert might suggest this wasn't a great strategy for the coming of the new kingdom; surely Jesus would have better things to be doing, more influential people to meet? He could have performed a dazzling miracle in front of a huge crowd, or preached up a storm to the masses. Instead he chose a walk.

He also could have healed the travellers' pain in an instant. 'Guys, it's OK. I'm Jesus and I'm fine! You don't need to rehash the events that have happened; you don't need to worry anymore.' Instead he chose to listen.

Cheryl Richardson rightly says, 'People start to heal the moment they feel heard.' I find that so hard to hold on to. The minute someone starts telling me a problem, my mind is whirring with solutions and ideas. I have to bite my tongue not to interrupt them with my brilliant suggestions. I remember one morning I came downstairs and my daughter Abigail was crying, wrapped in Diane's arms. 'What's wrong?' I asked. Diane told me Abi was upset about her nystagmus. I jumped in to fix-it mode and started explaining to Abi that new research was coming out all the time that might mean big changes in the future, and that, in the meantime, we could buy some extra equipment to help her at school. This seemed like kindness to me, to offer a solution to a problem, but Diane said, 'She doesn't want to be fixed right now, she just needs her dad to love her and listen.'

I've got a way to go on this, but I'm keen to learn what it means to 'hold space' for people. I love this definition from author Heather Plett: 'It means that we are willing to walk alongside another person in whatever journey they're on without judging them, making them feel inadequate, trying to fix them, or trying to impact the outcome. When we hold space for other people, we open our hearts, offer unconditional support, and let go of judgement and control.'[6] This is something that we at Kintsugi Hope know to be incredibly important as we build supportive relationships with people. We don't need to have all the answers but we can make a huge difference by listening without judgment.

Sadly, my inbox is full of people who have had others respond to their pain in incredibly unhelpful ways. One lady came to talk to me after I'd spoken on depression and said she had been crying every day for months and couldn't stop.

When she told her pastor what had been happening and that she was worried she might have depression, he said, 'I hear no faith in that statement.' When I gently suggested she might find it helpful to see her GP, tears rolled down her face. 'Really? Doesn't that mean I have failed?' I wish that was an isolated story.

Over the last few years I've done a number of tours on the back of my books, speaking around the country about the themes and giving people space to explore them through a talk, music and more. At the end of each evening we make space for anyone who wants to come and talk. Occasionally people will look to us as though we can solve all their problems, but, nine times out of ten, they just want someone to listen without judging.

On the road to Emmaus, Jesus modelled that there can be a healthy space for journeying pain and grief together without trying to fill in the blanks and answer all the questions. Sometimes it's simply better to say, 'I'm sorry you're in pain', than try to offer any solution. In the hopes of trying to make things better, we sometimes say the words 'at least'. 'At least they're not suffering any more', when we've lost a person we love to cancer. 'At least you have two other children', as Ellen was told when her longed for baby died. 'At least you're young and you've got time to meet someone else', when a relationship breaks down. When we try to find a silver lining, we are trying to downgrade someone's suffering, and that rarely helps. Kindness is sitting with someone in their pain and not offering platitudes. It means not rushing on, not trying to push them to feel better when they're not ready and being committed to walk alongside them in that journey.

We can offer platitudes with the best intentions like, 'God will not give you more than you can handle', 'Everything happens for a reason' and 'What doesn't kill you makes you stronger'. Again, they rarely help. Matt Haig in his book *Reasons to Stay Alive* comments, 'What doesn't kill you very often makes you weaker. What doesn't kill you can leave you limping for the rest of your days. What doesn't kill you can make you scared to leave your house, or even your bedroom, and have you trembling, or mumbling incoherently, or leaning with your head on a windowpane, wishing you could return to the time before the thing that didn't kill you.'[7]

Kate Bowler was a London-born theology professor. She was doing really well in her job, was married to her school sweetheart and they had a newborn son. Then she was then diagnosed with stage IV colon cancer. In her book *Everything Happens for a Reason and Other Lies I've Loved*, she gives some advice on things to say to someone who is struggling:

- I'd love to bring you a meal this week, can I email you about it?
- You are a beautiful person.
- I am so grateful to hear about how you are doing and just want you to know I am on your team.
- Can I give you a hug?
- Oh, my friend, that sounds hard.
- Silence.[8]

We can all do this. Our world is full of loneliness, but we can all listen to someone and we all need someone to listen to us. There is no 'them and us'. When it comes to mental wellbeing, there is no such thing as people who are in need and people who aren't; we're all in this together. We need to create spaces and relationships where we can each tell our stories freely. I love the term 'feeling felt', a phrase coined by professor Dan Siegel, which describes what happens in our minds where we share stories and feel truly present to one another.[9] Author K.J. Ramsey comments, 'The more we share our stories and are received with compassion, the more our brains are shaped to anticipate love instead of rejection. When we allow others to bear witness to our own weakness, we learn to relate to ourselves with kindness and hope. When someone listens and validates us as we tell our story they ignite a new way of considering our story – as valuable, worth hearing, worth telling, worth living.'[10]

On the road to Emmaus, Jesus started telling a story – the bigger story of God's love for his people revealed through the prophets. No doubt he would have gone through Isaiah and talked about 'the man of sorrow' and referenced Psalm 22, 'My God, why have you forsaken me?' The travellers would have been aware of these scriptures but never thought the person Jesus was describing in them was the man listening and journeying with them at that moment. He challenged their version of the story to help them face reality, linking his story to theirs. They needed to know they were part of this story and that God had been working his plans out all along. They were included – and so are we – in this great story of how God gets his family back.

They persuaded Jesus to have a meal with them, and as Jesus broke the bread with these exhausted and hopeless travellers, Clopas recognised him. Suddenly it all made sense! Christ had died but he had come back to life; death itself has been defeated! Luke is showing us the first meal of this new creation. The first meal in Genesis brought a curse; this meal was about entering into new beginnings. Jesus took the bread, blessed it and broke it and their eyes were opened to the signs of this new world. A world where the intimacy of eating with God was possible because of what Jesus had done, a world where the barrier between humans and God had gone.

THE INNER CRITIC

Some of us find it far easier to be kind to others than to ourselves. Research says that we have anything between 12,000 and 60,000 thoughts a day, and roughly 80% of these are negative.[11] But we also know that having positive thoughts leads to positive emotions, which can help us improve our overall resilience.[12]

Over the years I have come to recognise that I am my own worst enemy. My inner critic is loud and constantly tells me that I have fallen short, I should try harder and I don't have enough discipline. There is nothing off limits, nowhere the inner critic won't go, and the voice is always accusing and aggressive. No grace, no love, no kindness, no compassion. When you listen to your inner critic it reduces your ability to take risks as you don't want to give that voice the opportunity to tell you that you shouldn't have bothered because you only messed it up. The inner critic loves to compare you with others, pointing out how much more confident, capable and clever they are than you.

Certain situations are trigger points for the inner critic to become more vocal. I've realised for me one of these is reading out loud. There were a numbers of times at school when I was asked to read out loud in class or assembly and stumbled over some words or completely mispronounced them. Of course, the other pupils all laughed, so now, while I have no problem speaking on TV in front of millions, I still hate reading anything in front of even five other people as my inner critic can't wait to tell me what a fool I am. The inner critic takes something that we may struggle with and turns it into our weakness and then our identity. 'You can't read in public, you're useless. How old are you?'

The difference between a self-critical person and a person who shows self-acceptance is that the latter doesn't fall apart when they make a mistake, they just see it as part of life, something they can learn from. Researchers have found that self-acceptance is key to life satisfaction, and yet most of us struggle to do it. Many say they are good at being kind to other people but 'when asked to rate how often they were kind to themselves, almost half gave themselves a rating of five or less out of ten. Only a handful of respondents – 5 per cent – rated themselves as a ten on self-acceptance'.[13]

Diane shows a video as part of our Kintsugi Hope groups where women talk about the horrible things they say to themselves, things they would never say to anyone else. It highlights how damaging and unfair this voice is by asking those same women to say those negative things to a picture of themselves as a child. Of course they can't. Instead of focusing in on their failings like their inner critic, they choose to highlight the positives and say well done for the ways they're trying. Though it's a powerful video, I didn't think it had much relevance to me. But I was at my parent's house the day after the first time I saw it, and I saw a picture of me at the age of 4, and suddenly it made sense. God really spoke to me, challenging the way I often speak to myself. Listening to your inner critic is exhausting. They tell you you're not enough, to try harder, to do more. So I'm trying. I'm not perfect – as my inner critic will say! – but I'm trying. I've learnt to recognise that voice and I have realised I don't have to believe it. Instead, I need to find the gap between stimulus and action and remind myself:

- You are doing the best you can.
- Making a mistake doesn't make you a failure.
- Struggling doesn't make you a failure – it makes you human.
- No one is perfect.
- It's OK not to be OK all the time.
- It's also OK that not everyone will like you.
- Everyone is allowed a bad day.

Being super critical doesn't serve us. It doesn't help us to be a better person because people who listen to this voice are more likely to brood and less likely to move towards a resolution where one is required. We need to demonstrate self-compassion and speak to ourselves as we would speak to someone we love and cherish. We also need to continually speak God's truth over ourselves. This is what he says:

- You are loved with an everlasting love (Jer. 31:3).
- He rejoices over you with singing and dancing (Zeph. 3:17).
- You are fearfully and wonderfully made (Psa. 139:14).
- You are a child of God (Rom. 8:16).

How about the next time our inner critic gets noisy, we remind it of some of these amazing truths?

BOUNDARIES

I used to think that the most kind and compassionate people in the world were the ones who just gave endlessly and never seemed to have any needs of their own. I now realise that's not the case. People like Mother Teresa, who had a phenomenal ability to give, actually have lots of boundaries in their lives. Mother Teresa had a very strict routine of prayer, worship and rest, and I'm sure these enabled her to do all the amazing work she did.

As I young person growing up in church culture, there was a huge focus on mission as something we went and did and less about lifestyle choices we could make daily. I jumped around in worship to *History Maker*, believing I could change the world. Then I tried and got exhausted and disillusioned. John Mark Comer points out in his book *The Ruthless Elimination of Hurry* that limitations are good for us but somehow, both inside and outside of the church, that isn't always a popular message. He comments, 'Doesn't really have the ring of a *New York Times* bestseller does it? *Accepting Your Limitations: How to Make Peace with Your Mortality and Cosmic Insignificance.*'[14] Yet the reality is we are all limited in what we can do, and realising that is, for me at least, a relief. We are limited by time – we all have a finite number of hours in the day, and none of us are going to live forever. We are limited in terms of our abilities – we don't all have the same brains or bodies. We all have different personal circumstances – I have four kids and loving them well means I don't want to be away from them all the time, which puts limits on my time and ability to travel. Accepting our limitations is a sign of maturity not weakness.

We need to set our own boundaries too. Kindness, I have come to realise, is not being a doormat or allowing people unlimited access. Sometimes, if we're not careful, we can resort to doing whatever it takes to make others happy, no matter how badly they might treat us. As Brené Brown discovered in her research, 'The most compassionate people I interviewed also have the most well-defined and well-respected boundaries. It surprised me at the time, but now I get it. They assume that other people are doing the best they can, but they also ask for what they need, and they don't put up with a lot of crap. Compassionate people ask for what they need. They say no when they need to, and when they say yes, they mean it. They're compassionate because their boundaries keep them out of resentment.'[15]

WHO ARE YOU IN THE STORY?

If you asked someone which story in the Bible best describes kindness, many would answer: The Good Samaritan. We hear it as early as Sunday school, when we acted it out, remembering its message of being kind to those who are not like you, even to people you may despise. The message we hear is 'be like the Samaritan who rescues the poor man who has been beaten and left with no dignity'. Like many, I naturally assume God is asking me to be the character in the story who is the rescuer, the Good Samaritan. But Rev Sam Wells suggests we have been looking at this story the wrong way round and that our western mindset has a big part to play in the way we interpret these stories. He says:

We are *not* the Samaritan. *We are the man by the side of the road.* We are the one who is stripped, we are the one who is bruised, we are the one who is half-dead. This is how we begin to reflect on questions of compassion and good deeds and social justice. We are the needy ones. We long for relationship, we long for forgiveness, we long for reconciliation, we long for eternal life. And we'd be happy to accept these things from the priest or the Levite. These are people who seem like ourselves, people from our own social background. They have security. They have social esteem. They have resources. But the story is telling us those people can't help us. They can't give us what we so desperately need.[16]

This brought me up short. Am I willing to accept kindness from people I don't know? People I have judged and put down? Will I let go of my pride and receive help? Wells goes on to say that the Good Samaritan in the story is not us, it's Jesus. When we were broken, beaten, ashamed and had lost our way, he came to us. Maybe the story is more about accepting our own brokenness. The kindness we see in Christ is an example of how we are to share his kindness to others, not as the rescuer but as someone who sees Jesus in the faces of those around us. We don't see charity cases but people who are human beings made in the image of God, people who have as much to teach us about being human as we do them.

Some of us find accepting kindness really hard. Someone pays us a compliment and we bat it away immediately. Someone tries to help us and we feel uncomfortable and try to put them off. We should get curious and ask ourselves why. Do we feel like we don't deserve kindness and help? Does it mean that we'd have to surrender some sort of control? Or lose our pride? Receiving something is an act of vulnerability and it's all too easy to keep a wall up which robs both us and the giver.

Dieter F. Uchtdorf, a leader in the Church of Jesus Christ of Latter-day Saints in Germany, says, 'Every gift that is offered to us—especially a gift that comes from the heart—is an opportunity to build or strengthen a bond of love. When we are good and grateful receivers, we open a door to deepen our relationship with the giver of the gift. But when we fail to appreciate or even reject a gift, we not only hurt those who extend themselves to us, but in some way we harm ourselves as well.'[17]

I believe kindness has the potential to change the world, to change us as people. I want to be known as a kind person, someone who considers others. It isn't the most glamourous of adjectives; it sometimes seems more exciting to be described as adventurous, funny, creative or clever, but the world has never needed kindness more. Social media has desensitised us towards each other in many ways. People think nothing of writing a scathing attack on someone in the public eye because of their performance or personal views. We've forgotten that a real human being reads those comments. A human being, made in the image of God, who is trying their best, making mistakes just like us, who hurts in the same way we hurt. Before we could hide behind our mobile phones, we didn't run up to others and shout and belittle them. We would never say to someone's face the things that are regularly written online.

As we face an uncertain future I want to choose kindness, compassion and forgiveness for my own sake as well as for the sake of others. The best thing we can do for our own wellbeing is to care for others, to give ourselves to more than our own self-interests. That is how we become fully human.

CHAPTER 9

GRITTY GRATITUDE

I am naturally a glass half-empty person. The good thing about that is it means I have a natural pull towards working out what is wrong with the world so I can be part of helping make it right. What's not so great is that gratitude doesn't come easily to me. It doesn't help that our culture wants to make us feel dissatisfied with what we already have in order to provoke us to go after more. Advertisers try to sell us happiness in a bottle or a brand. We're constantly told we don't have enough and that we need more in order to make us happy, but we also know that when happiness is attached to accumulation of more things, it is often short-lived. Kristi Nelson, Executive Director of A Network for Grateful Living, challenges my thinking when using the analogy of a glass being half-full or half-empty. The key, she points out, is being grateful for the glass. Yes, at times it may feel half-full when life is good and other times when life is very tough it can feel almost empty, but the key to gratitude is to realise that you have life, and life in itself is a gift. She writes, 'Being grateful for simply having a glass is key because without it, half of anything wouldn't matter. Without it, life would either be a puddle or thin air. The glass is a container for our experiences – all experience – and some people seem to know that noticing and being grateful for this container dwarfs everything and can turn any and all contents in our favour.'[1]

Gratitude is a choice, and it needs to be cultivated like a muscle that grows and develops. It's a healthy habit that, when practised, helps us cultivate resilience. Henri Nouwen comments,

> I always thought of gratitude as a spontaneous response to the awareness of gifts received, but now I realize that gratitude can be also lived as a discipline. The discipline of gratitude is the explicit effort to acknowledge that all I am and have is given to me as a gift of love, a gift to be celebrated with joy. Gratitude as a discipline involves a conscious choice. I can choose to be grateful even when my emotions and feelings are still steeped in hurt and resentment. It is amazing how many occasions present themselves in which I can choose gratitude instead of complaint.[2]

Again, I want to stress that I'm not talking about glossing over the hard stuff. Being grateful doesn't mean that we're not facing challenges or dealing with devastating loss and pain.

We're talking about gritty gratitude, an attitude that we work on and deploy with effort, knowing that being grateful doesn't cancel out the very real and very painful things in our lives, but allows us to realise that there are good things all around us too.

My favourite definition of gratitude is from psychologist Karen Reivich, who says we should 'hunt the good stuff'. She encourages us to actively search out positive aspects of something.[3] Some days it may feel like you have to hunt really hard, but it's worth it. Research shows that the health benefits of practising gratitude are staggering. Being thankful can:

- increase happiness, reduce depression and strengthen resilience;
- reduce blood pressure and chronic pain;
- increase energy;
- help us to live longer;
- improve our self-esteem and our empathy;
- help us to sleep better.

How? Much like practising kindness, gratitude actually rewires our brains, helping to start the production of dopamine and serotonin, the hormones which make us feel content and happy.[4] Gratitude can block toxic emotions like envy, resentment and regret, and help us to be resilient to life's most stressful events including trauma and suffering. Practising gratitude will also help us recover faster and reduce the likelihood of anxiety and PTSD.[5]

Gratitude brings joy. Brené Brown says that in 12 years of research, with over 11,000 pieces of data, she has never interviewed anyone who would describe themselves as joyful who didn't actively practise gratitude.[6] As theologian David Steindl-Rast said, 'It is not joy that makes us grateful, it is gratitude that makes us joyful.'[7]

GIVING THANKS IN THE TOUGH PLACES

The Psalms show us how we can hold the tension between acknowledging our pain and still thanking God for his goodness.

Psalm 13 says:

> How long, Lord? Will you forget me forever?
>> How long will you hide your face from me?
> How long must I wrestle with my thoughts
>> and day after day have sorrow in my heart?
>> How long will my enemy triumph over me?
> Look on me and answer, Lord my God.
>> Give light to my eyes, or I will sleep in death,
> and my enemy will say, 'I have overcome him,'
>> and my foes will rejoice when I fall.
> But I trust in your unfailing love;
>> my heart rejoices in your salvation.
> I will sing the Lord's praise,
>> for he has been good to me.

Here, David is crying out to God, and he doesn't hide the fact that he feels like he's been forgotten and that his enemies are winning. Somehow – in the midst of these feelings that are clearly overwhelming him – he gives praise to God. His heart rejoices in his salvation and, despite the circumstances, he can say 'God has been good to me'.

I have spent some time in Iraq, learning from charities who are supporting refugees, and there I heard so many harrowing stories of people being persecuted for their faith. I can't even imagine the tension and fear of living in such a culture. I was taken to what was little more than an underground cave, which is where people used to meet and worship God. It was dark, with barely any light coming from the outside, but this is what the church called home. As I stood there, I closed my eyes and tried to picture these beautiful people singing songs to God when they knew the police could be outside. They refused to stop meeting and refused to stop worshipping their God. For them, Jesus was always worth praising, no matter their circumstances and no matter the cost.

Another place that had a huge impact on me is Guyana, which I visited to try to understand more of black culture and to support churches in dealing with issues of violence. Guyana is the poorest country in South America. The murder rate is three times that of the United States, and there are ever increasing reports of kidnapping, shootings, carjackings, home invasions and violent robberies. As we drove to a church to speak at a midweek meeting, I could see the bullet holes in many of the wooden houses; we were told there had been a gunfight the night before.

There were ditches in the road which made driving very difficult, dug by local thieves in order to make cars slow down so they could rob them more easily. I arrived at the church and quickly realised they didn't have enough money to finish building it. The centre was like a large sandpit. They had the most awful PA system that crackled and spat out feedback; their instruments were limited to dustbin lids as drums. I knew the congregation were dealing with a lot. Many of the women had been left alone to bring up their children as their husbands had disappeared. Some families had lost more than one child to drugs and crime. The Christians were a minority in a community divided between Hindus and Muslims. I have been to lots of poor communities but for me this was one of the most challenging. I felt for the single mums, and struggled not to feel hopeless about the limited job prospects, the tension due to crime, and the fear of a group of violent men who had recently escaped from the prison and were causing chaos.

Yet, as the service began, the first song they sang was *Jesus, Lover of My Soul*. I will never forget it. Even though the PA was giving me a splitting headache and, if I am honest, none of it sounded very good musically, it was one of the most beautiful things I have ever heard. The sincerity and the passion was raw, a gut-wrenching cry to God as they sang:

I love you
I need you
Though my world may fall

I'll never let you go
My Saviour
My closest friend
I will worship you
I will worship you until the very end

I could feel myself getting very emotional. It was one of the most humbling experiences of my life. Despite the multiple challenges this community faced, they understood gratitude. They praised God for who he is, they thanked their Saviour for dying on the cross and for giving them a sense of hope, purpose and belief that change is possible. The smiles, the dancing, the tears will stay with me for the rest of my life; a beautiful and broken people giving praise to their God no matter what.

My friends Will van der Hart and Dr Rob Waller say, 'Biblical gratitude is not conditional upon positive circumstances, but is an attitude of the heart that exists regardless of either life's ease or life's hardships.'[8] While Henri Nouwen describes gratitude as a quality of the heart 'that allows us to live joyfully and peacefully even though our struggle continue'.[9] When life is at its toughest for me, I try to sing *Jesus, Lover of My Soul*, remembering the example of the church in Guyana. I remind myself that my heart needs to be soft and appreciative, and try to be thankful that, whatever I go through, I am not alone and never will be.

I have seen this incredible attitude in maximum security prisons, rehab centres, the underground church in Asia and in some of the world's poorest places. I am always moved when I worship with people who have lost so much – their freedoms have been taken away, their health is failing, their future is uncertain – but their love for Jesus is huge and inspiring.

WORSHIP BEHIND BARS

We see this example in the Early Church too. When people talk about the Early Church, it's often wishing we could be more like them in terms of their passion for community and for the poor. I don't imagine any of us would wish to sign up for the persecution and the suffering they went through. It was a complex world, ruled by the Romans who had many gods and shrines everywhere. These gods were involved in every part of life, both public and private, and during festivals the gods had to been acknowledged and kept happy. Jewish people were not forced to worship Greek gods in the same way that non-Jewish people were, but speaking out against them was not allowed. As well as living in a difficult culture, much of Paul's hardship came through misunderstandings and relationship breakdowns from within the church; arguments around the Gentiles turning to Christ and if they had the same rights as Jewish people. He also, famously, had a 'thorn in the flesh' (2 Cor. 12:7), was abandoned by all his friends while imprisoned (2 Tim. 1:15) and reached a point where he 'despaired of life itself' (2 Cor. 1:8). Paul also had relational problems with Barnabas over Mark, which left their relationship broken, and even Jesus' own followers questioned him.

One of the stories about Paul that has always stood out to me, is when he and Silas were in Philippi and were arrested after Paul commanded a spirit to leave a fortune-telling slave girl. Her owners weren't happy, so after Paul and Silas were put in front of a magistrate, they wound up in prison. They were stripped and beaten. Tom Wright describes what prisons were like back then: 'No provision was made for the prisoner's welfare. They had to rely on friends and family to bring them food and other necessities. Sanitation would be minimal; rodents and other vermin would be normal. The company would not be one's first choice of friends. A few days in such a hole might well make one hope for almost any punishment, a heavy fine, or banishment at least. If only one could get out of the horrid place.'[10]

The text tells us they were held in stocks (Acts 16:24), which could mean they were bound to a piece of wood by their feet. The positioning would have forced them to lie back on a cold floor, on their wounded and beaten flesh, which would have increased their suffering further still.[11] Yet it was right there that Paul and Silas prayed and sang hymns to God (Acts 16:25). Many believe they were singing the psalms; words that have been sung during some of the darkest times in history. Despite their suffering, they showed their gratitude to God, their appreciation and thankfulness for who he is. As they worshipped there was an earthquake, which not only set them free but led to the jailor coming to salvation, along with his household.

This shows me again that gratitude is a gutsy thing to do. Giving thanks to God in challenging circumstances reminds us that circumstances don't have complete hold on us, and they can't change our attitude unless we allow them to. After my two leg operations I had months lying in bed. There was little by way of the big and spectacular God moments going on, but I began to see him more and more in the little things. Ann Voskamp, author of *One Thousand Gifts*, says, 'When I give thanks for the seemingly microscopic, I make a place for God to grow within me.'[12] When we stop waiting for a huge life moment to be grateful (a new house or job, the birth of a child) and start looking to the little things, there's no end to the gifts we'll find are all around us. A message from a friend, a beautiful sunset, a delicious dinner, a good night's sleep, a moment of quiet in a usually busy house, a colleague who helps us solve a problem, our favourite show on TV... the list is endless.

When our problems are overwhelming, gratitude helps us change our perspective. One illustration that speaks to me on a near daily basis is when you see lifeless, grey concrete slabs on the ground but you spot tufts of grass or little flowers that have broken through and are straining towards the light. Despite the inhospitable environment and everything being against it, the grass will always grow again. Leave it there long enough, it might even crack the concrete. I want to be someone who sees the greyness of life – people's pain and their experience – but who also spots the life growing through the cracks. I want to see the possibilities of change and growth. I want to live a life of gratitude that says, no matter how hard life gets, there is always hope. I want to learn to shift my perspective from what I don't have, to what I do.

General Robbie Risner spent seven years as a prisoner of war in Vietnam. To help him cope he developed a habit of getting up at 5am, and would begin the day looking through a vent below the floor of the cell, watching insects crawling up blades of grass. Even in the midst of a prisoner war camp, he managed to be grateful for nature, which spoke to him of new life.[13] Gratitude constantly challenges our perspective. As Joshua Choonmin Kang said, 'Gratitude is the ability to have hope in the midst of seeming hopelessness. Gratitude isn't a drug to escape or ignore the reality of desperate circumstances. Instead, it gives us courage to confront our problems, offering hope where hope cannot be found.'[14]

SLOWING DOWN AND CELEBRATING

So if we're sold on the necessity and benefits of gratitude, how do we actually practise it? How do we build that muscle? The first thing I think we need to do is slow down.

We live at such a fast pace that our minds are never still. We reach for our phones the second we have a moment of space, whether it's in the queue at the checkout or waiting for a friend at a restaurant. We even reach for it when our mind is already occupied, say, when we're watching TV. We barely give ourselves a moment's break. In *The Ruthless Elimination of Hurry*, John Mark Corner comments,

'A recent study found that the average iPhone user touches his or her phone 2,617 times a day. Each user is on his or her phone for two and a half hours over seventy-six sessions, and that's for *all* smartphone users. Another study on millennials puts the number as twice that.'[15]

Every moment is taken up, from when we wake up till we go to sleep, but to truly appreciate something, you need to stop and take your time. An obvious example is that you can't appreciate a piece of art by looking at it for a couple of seconds then moving onto the next thing. We might take a moment to think 'I like that', but if we employ the art critic's thinking, exploring the skill, the creativity, the uniqueness, the textures, the colours, the time and effort that went into it, I'm sure we'd appreciate it a lot more. We live life at a constantly accelerated pace, rushing from one thing to another, often recognising that it's unsustainable and yet trying to do it anyway.

Gratitude challenges us to a change in lifestyle. To stop and smell the roses, to savour the good things of the past and the present, and to enjoy the anticipation of the future. It invites us to pause and think about God's nature – not just thanking him for what he gives us but taking time to sit in awe of his majesty. Slowing down helps us to live out of our values and take time to see things the way Jesus does. Jesus doesn't ask us to follow a set of rules, he asks us to become more like him. And as *The Message* translates Matthew 11:29, Jesus says, 'Walk with me and work with me—watch how I do it. Learn the unforced rhythms of grace.'

Gratitude invites us to celebrate, taking time to notice and appreciate the great things in our lives. I know that as soon as a good thing has happened or been achieved, I'm guilty of looking forwards to the next thing without taking time to appreciate what's happened. Some of that comes from a fear of taking too much pride in an achievement, or being perceived as being proud, but I believe God wants us to pause and rejoice when good things happen in the same way he wants us to pause and grieve over the painful things. God sets us the example by rejoicing over us: Zephaniah 3:17 says, 'The LORD your God is with you, the Mighty Warrior who saves. He will take great delight in you; in his love he will no longer rebuke you, but will rejoice over you with singing.' It's hard to imagine, but *God rejoices over us with signing*. He paused during creation to say what he'd made was good and he takes time to rejoice in us and enjoy us. You don't read anywhere in the Bible that God wants us to pray quickly and then leave him in peace; he wants us to pause so we can love him and be loved by him.

GETTING PRACTICAL

There are many ways to build an attitude of gratitude, but here are some simple suggestions you might like to try.

- Keep a journal where you list three things you're thankful for each day before you go to sleep.
- Take time over the dinner table to allow each person to say one thing they're thankful for.

- Take a breath before asking God for anything, then thank him for something he's already done and for who he is.
- Start making a list of 1,000 things you're grateful for. Write it down in a journal or on your phone and see how quickly you get to the 1,000 mark.
- Take a photo every day of something or someone you appreciate.
- Tell friends, family and work colleagues something you appreciate about them.
- Tell yourself things you appreciate about yourself!
- Build celebrations in to your personal, family and work rhythms, taking time to savour accomplishments, big and small.

Some of these things may feel slightly awkward and forced to start with but the more often we practice the habit of thankfulness, the easier it will become. Soon we'll be able to 'give thanks in all circumstances' (1 Thes. 5:18), as Paul encouraged the Thessalonians, aware of and enjoying the many gifts God gives us each and every day.

CHAPTER 10

GO GENTLY

One of the most helpful analogies for me on resilience was in a talk by holistic medicine pioneer and local GP, Professor Patrick Pietroni. He said, 'Being well and healthy is a bit like rowing a boat. Illness or other kind of problems can be thought of as crashing into a rock. Most approaches to tackle difficulties tend to focus on the rock... But the problem, or rock, is only half the story. The water level represents our background level of resilience. When we're feeling good in ourselves, with our emotional reserves at a high level, we may float over the rocks that on a bad day we'd hit. When we're feeling depleted, our water levels low, we're more likely to crash.'[1]

What keeps your water level high? What brings it lower? There will probably be some common ground for most of us, such as lack of sleep, a stressful situation at work or home, a bad diet, and being too busy can lower the water level, while rest, relaxation and healthy relationships can help bring it back up. There are of course other things that are more personal to us as individuals that bring us life. I found it really helpful to sit down and write some of these things out to get some concrete ideas on what helps me and what hinders me. What brings my resilience levels low is being tired, working too hard and listening to my inner critic. Some of the things that raise my resilience levels are self-compassion, exercise, prayer and safe relationships. Relationships that aren't as safe definitely fall into the category of things that deplete me and I've had to learn that sometimes you have to let go of relationships that aren't working.

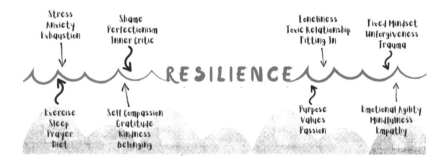

When I started recognising this, my first thought was that it didn't feel very Christian. Surely in order to love everyone, I need to be friends with everyone. But while we're called to love each other, and there is something holy about committed relationships that stay the course, I realised that my mindset was coming from a place of insecurity rather than a calling from God. We can't be friends with absolutely everyone because we don't have the time, and some relationships become toxic and draining and that needs addressing. Loving someone does not mean allowing them to treat us badly. Loving ourselves does not mean letting go of healthy boundaries and repeatedly putting ourselves in painful situations. There will be times when you've done everything you can to make something work and you need a break.

This is true of friendship and it's also true of jobs. My good friend Cathy Madavan has written a brilliant book on resilience called *Irresistible*. She says that 'while endurance is essential, there is a point where we acknowledge that it's time to call it a day. There are times where we have to admit and accept that letting go, drawing a line, or walking away are just as admirable and possibly just as brave as staying'.[2]

Leaving XLP was heart-wrenching for me. Sacrifice, sweat and tears had been poured into the charity for many years and it was a place that gave me some wonderful friendships and memories. As I surrendered to God I was reminded of this: 'Getting to the next level always requires ending something, leaving it behind, and moving on. Growth itself demands that we move on. Without the ability to end things, people stay stuck, never becoming who they are meant to be, never accomplishing all that their talents and abilities should afford them.'[3] This quote rang so true, reminding me that even if it felt strange to leave things behind, it was so important I did, in order to be able to embrace what was ahead.

LETTING GO OF SHAME

Shame is another key factor that can hold us back and keep our resilience level low. It is pervasive, spreading its lies that we are not good enough, that we are to blame and should have more faith or a better attitude in our difficulties, that we and our lives should be perfect. Shame drives perfectionism, which can cause crippling anxiety. Unlike guilt, it doesn't propel us towards healthy change, rather it makes us feel that there is something wrong with us. I found myself stuck in a cycle where my shame drove my perfectionism, which drove my anxiety, which played its part in driving my depression.

Will van der Hart and Dr Rob Waller, who wrote *The Power of Belonging*, say, 'Shame-bound leaders appear "nearly perfect" to those around them. They present brilliantly, work diligently, and serve humbly. They may even talk about community and authenticity. They don't look broken to those around them, but they are broken to themselves. They may feel like frauds or suffer from low self-esteem and be plagued by embarrassment, defensiveness. They may suppress these feelings in activity and overwork but feel deeply lonely. They might even feel secure in the perception of others but not in self-perception.'[4]

Donald Capps, an American pastoral theologian, says that shame is the feeling of being 'disgusted, disappointed or disillusioned with oneself'.[5] It's a judgment – not of what you do, but of who you are. So it encourages you to stay quiet so others don't find out. It needs secrecy to stay alive;

it can't stand to be spoken about.

My lovely friends Heather Churchill and Clare Musters wrote a brilliant book on shame, and they have a wonderful ability to take complex issues and make them accessible. They point out that it's helpful to picture the hippocampus (the part of the limbic system involved in regulating emotions and storing memories) as a number of filing cabinets of memories in the brain. 'One "filing cabinet" holds "normal" memories that have generally been processed and are easily remembered. However, another "filing cabinet" stores traumatic memories of events that we frequently don't want to think about because they are frightening, painful and/or shameful. In this "filing cabinet" the memories can remain unprocessed because they are so distressing to remember that we try to avoid thinking of them.'[6]

Shame is the opposite of the way God longs for us to live. When Adam and Eve sinned in the garden, their shame didn't stop God looking for them and pursuing them. Whenever Jesus encountered shame he ministered straight into it. One great example is Zacchaeus (Luke 19:1–10), who was considered a traitor to his own people. He was despised and rejected for having sold out to the Roman authorities. The traditional understanding of the story is that he was small and so he had to go up the tree to see Jesus. This may be the case, but perhaps what also made him climb the tree that day was his shame and his need to be away from everyone who would judge him. Interestingly, Jesus dealt with his shame before his guilt by asking to come to his house for tea. In that culture, to have a meal with someone was an intimate affair, reserved for family and close friends. Having met with Jesus, Zacchaeus confessed his guilt and promised to give away his money to the poor.

The antidote to shame is understanding and empathy, and that is what we find when we bring it to Jesus. Getting professional help at the right time is also incredibly helpful and there's info in the back of this book on finding a good counsellor in your area. Many of the issues we've looked at in *Bouncing Forwards* also work to combat shame, especially self-compassion, belonging and finding safe relationships.

Mindfulness is also very helpful in dealing with shame and building resilience. It asks you to notice your thoughts without judging them. Some Christians have concerns about mindfulness due to its apparent roots in Buddhism, but mindfulness can be seen in the teaching of Jesus: 'Give your entire attention to what God is doing right now, and don't get worked up about what may or may not happen tomorrow. God will help you deal with whatever hard things come up when the time comes' (Matt. 6:34, *The Message*).

If you've ever tried to just ignore those unhelpful thoughts that come into your mind, or change them to be something positive, you'll know it never works. Instead, some mindfulness experts suggest seeing your thoughts like trains running through the station of your mind. When a thought seems to have parked itself for a while and is causing some problems, they suggest not running from it, judging it or trying to change it. Instead, take the time to notice it. Even if it makes you feel uncomfortable, those feelings will pass. As you examine a thought, it too will pass.[7]

THE SHADOW

Once we step out of shame we can begin to examine and take responsibility for what Peter Scazzero describes as our shadow side. 'Your shadow is the accumulation of untamed emotions, less-than pure motives and thoughts that, while largely unconscious, strongly influence and shape your behaviours. It is the damaged but mostly hidden version of who you are.'[8] This shadow may show up in obvious ways such as anger, jealousy, resentment and greed, or more subtly in needing to rescue others, overworking, needing to be liked by other people or rigidity.

Scazzero talks about how our gifts, that are good, have shadow sides to them. I've seen this personally, and there is such a fine line between strengths and weaknesses. I want to do things excellently, which is a good thing, but the flip side is slipping into perfectionism. That doesn't serve me well and can also mean I put unfair expectations on others too. I am empathetic but if I'm not careful that can lead to emotional burnout. I'm sure you can apply this to your own strengths.

Our shadows are the damaged versions of who we are; they are the behaviours we use to protect ourselves from actually changing. We keep them hidden because they make us feel so vulnerable. Every now and then, circumstances reveal them to us and we can see more clearly what's going on. I love speaking to groups of people but having to stop that because of COVID-19 meant I realised how much I relied on the affirmation and encouragement I would usually receive afterwards. Now, I can finish recording a talk and that's it, there's no one there to tell me if it went well or badly. But it has been so helpful for me to reflect on my motives; my desire should always be to serve God and not my ego.

Self-awareness is key in developing resilience. The more we're able to reflect on our own strengths and shadows, the more whole we can become. And the good news is we don't have to muster up the energy to change. God sees us as partners not puppets; our willingness to bring our brokenness and vulnerability before him is the key. He can change us. It is Christ in us that is the hope of glory, not our ability to make things happen. If we are willing to surrender to him, he will come and meet us in whatever we are facing.

IT'S NOT ABOUT TRYING HARDER

We sometimes see God as a behaviourist, checking up on us all the time, but God didn't sacrifice his beloved Son just to be cross with us and tell us to 'try harder'. The early Christians in Galatia were falling into this trap of believing they somehow had to earn God's love through activity. Paul encouraged the church to see the flesh as the opposite to what the Spirit of God wants to do in our lives. The flesh says we are better off living independent of God and we can attain everything through human effort. The reality is God created us with a desire to be loved and to feel worth. God made us to be holy and blameless and it's by his Spirit that we know who we really are (Rom. 8:16). Ephesians 5:2 tells us, 'Mostly what God does is love you. Keep company with him and learn a life of love. Observe how Christ loved us. His love was not cautious but extravagant. He didn't love in order to get something from us but to give everything of himself to us' (*The Message*). We are precious in his sight.

When I was younger, I remember hearing lots of sermons on 'the flesh'. I used to think the flesh was the part of me that never wanted to get up early to have a two-hour quiet time, or the part of me that was stopping me witnessing to my friends. I just needed to pray harder, focus more and get my flesh nailed down in order to beat it. Greg Boyd, in his book *Seeing is Believing*, described it in a much more helpful way: 'Living in the flesh, then, is living in deception and thus in opposition to truth. It is living as though God is not who God really is, and we are not who the Bible says we really are. It is living to create worth, value and fulfilment in our own lives by what we can do, achieve or acquire on our own rather than freely receiving our worth, value and fulfilment from our creator.'[9]

We don't need to perform for God! At times, we try to earn his love through activity and that means we miss out on intimacy with him. He reveals his heart to us by his

Spirit, but we are often too busy to realise it because we're trying to earn his acceptance. We find it so hard to truly know that he loves us and that his love never changes no matter what happens in our lives and no matter what we do.

For me, the key is being willing to walk away from those habits that are so destructive in our lives to realise that, with the help of the Holy Spirit, it is possible to be free to embrace who we are truly meant to be. It is not easy and it is an ongoing process that we'll spend a lifetime working towards, but it is worth it. And that's why I want to end this book with encouraging you to go gently. You might have been expecting a more rousing finish to this book. A final exhortation to go forwards with grit and determination, overcoming setbacks and not letting anything get you down. But that's not what I want to leave you with. Think about this:

> Studies show that more often than not, the need
> to prove our worth and value and find significance,
> pushes us into busy-busy syndrome. These subtle
> drivers push us on to strive to do more. Sometimes
> through guilt, a fear of failure, not wanting to
> disappoint or wanting to meet other expectations,
> we push ourselves beyond our limits, taking on more
> than is good for us, extending ourselves to the points
> of exhaustion. The problem is that we can only live
> on adrenalin rushes for a certain amount of time. The
> highs and lows drain us of emotional energy and our

drivenness leads to exhaustion. With restlessness
and unease in our soul, the weight of weariness takes
its toll and life becomes a duty not a delight.[10]

Learning to accept ourselves in the midst of depression,
anxiety, questions and doubts is to accept that we are loved
with all our imperfections. We can rest in what God says
about us, knowing who he is and who we are, thanks to his
amazing love. As we've encouraged people to run Kintsugi
Hope groups around the country, we've realised that so
many people don't think they're good enough to do it. Many
of us think we have to be healed and sorted before our
experience is valuable or valid in the eyes of others. But the
truth is we are all wounded, and life isn't as straightforward
as to say 'we get hurt [right-pointing arrow] we heal [right-
pointing arrow] we help others'. Many times, we will need
to speak from our wounds not our scars, not waiting till we
perceive we're ready. None of us are perfect. We all have
strengths and weaknesses, and often our weaknesses
make us more empathetic and so can become strengths.

One of the most beautiful parts of the *Honesty Over
Silence* tour was seeing people embrace and celebrate
the fact that they are 'flawsome', ie 'an individual who
embraces their flaws and is awesome regardless'. We
are flawed and fallible but no less loved and wonderful
for it. At the end of each session, as a response to what
we'd discussed, we encourage each person to put their
thumbprint on the cross at the front as a sign that they
were worth dying for.

Author Brennan Manning says he thinks the first question God might ask when we meet him face to face would be, 'Did you believe I loved you?' How many of us truly live knowing we are truly loved? How might that change us if we knew a greater measure of our worth in God's eyes? Author Ann Voskamp says, 'Letting yourself be loved is an act of terrifying vulnerability and surrender, letting yourself be loved is its own kind of givenness. Letting yourself be loved gives you over to someone's mercy and leaves you trusting that they will keep loving you. That they will love you the way you want to be loved that won't break your heart.'[11]

So *go gently*. Be kind to yourself as you look to the things in your past and present that cause pain. Have the courage to step out of your shame and into God's love. Give space for your emotions, recognising they are important signals to you in working out how you are doing and when something needs to change. Take your time to process your trauma with a professional who you can trust to support you through the process. Show yourself some compassion when things go wrong and you make mistakes; speak to yourself the way you would speak to a best friend, with words of life wrapped in love and kindness. Go gently in your relationships, remembering we all need to feel safe and be listened to, and we don't need to bow to the pressure to fit in rather than truly belong. Make peace with the fact that life is never going to be perfect and that you can keep going regardless. Hunt for the good that's there even on the darkest days, and live in thankfulness for all you have.

Remember: you don't have to have this all figured out because not one single person on the planet does. All we can do is make daily choices to take a step in the right direction.

My prayer for you as you finish this book is borrowed from the words of a poet called Jane Smith. Jane has a rare form of blood cancer but she still manages to smile despite her pain. To me, she is a picture of resilience, thriving in the midst of huge adversity, and this poem is one of the most beautiful things I have ever read. I pray you will find:

Acceptance in the anguish
Beauty in the bruises
Belief in the brokenness
Breakthrough in the battle
Comfort in the conflict
Contentment in the confusion
Courage in the crisis
Determination in the distress
Diamonds in the dust
Dignity in the disappointment
Direction in the difficulty
Discovery in the darkness
Faith in the fear
Fortitude in the frustration
Grace in the grief
Healing in the horror
Hope in the hurt

Insight in the injury

Inspiration in the illness

Lessons in the living

Love in the loneliness

Mercy in the misunderstanding

Opportunity in the ordeal

Patience in the problems

Peace in the panic

Perseverance in the perplexity

Purpose in the pain

Refuge in the regrets

Rest in the restrictions

Sanctuary in the suffering

Serenity in the scars

Shelter in the shock

Stillness in the storm

Strength in the shadows

Support in the sadness

Treasure in the trials

Trust in the trauma

Victory in the vulnerability

Wisdom in the weakness[12]

AFTERWORD

As I reflect on the last six months, as we've been battling with Covid-19, I realise again how fragile we are. There is so much we have no control over. Learning to accept that is a daily challenge. I have discovered that accepting and facing challenging circumstances in my life is not defeat, rather it takes courage. I have realised that grief will come and hit me at unexpected moments and that's OK. It's normal. My desire to try to fit in everywhere has gone but my desire to belong as my authentic self is stronger as I see more of God in my brokenness. I embrace a healthy doubt, knowing that if one area of my life is tough, it doesn't have to affect absolutely everything else. I live with hope, knowing my future is wrapped up with the future of others and that God is always working to reconcile everything to himself. My pain is not wasted, yet that doesn't mean I don't suffer with the impact of past trauma, which rears its head particularly in times of stress. I'm so grateful God turns things around and uses our pain in amazing ways.

I've discovered a new passion to tell people how loved and special they are, made in the image of a loving God. I want them to know that there's nothing they can do or say that will change the love God has for them.

As I journey onwards, my unanswered questions still in my hands, I am trying to embrace the mystery. I hold on to the fact that I can't control my circumstances but I can decide how to respond to them. Success for me will be to live by my values, aligning them to Christ's values.

I want to bounce forwards, demonstrating emotional agility when my feelings are threatening to overwhelm me. As Jesus walked alongside his friends on the Emmaus road, I long to walk with friends in their pain. I don't want to jump in with judgmental opinions or a desire to fix them, but to truly listen and understand and to let them know they are not alone.

I know I need to keep my inner critic in check, watching how perfectionism can reveal itself in my life. I have to make my peace with the fact I will never be perfect but I can become more whole as a person and more comfortable in my own skin. I want to embrace my limitations and live a healthy pace of life.

Researching and writing this book has stretched me more than any of the ones I've written previously. I have drawn on so many different sources and am indebted to the wonderful minds of Susan David, Carol Dweck, Chris Johnstone, Brené Brown, Angela Duckworth and Martin Seligman. They, and so many others, have made years of research available in an accessible way for us. As I write these final words, I'm struck again by the fact that no matter how insightful psychology, how stretching theology and how inspirational activism, nothing beats knowing the one who made us. So I finish writing this book with a greater desire to know God more.

There are times I have got lost in my questions, my past experiences, the hurt and the pain. At times I feel like I am able to do little more than limp forwards, but, when everything is stripped back, I know I am child of God. I am loved. I tend to forget that sometimes and try to figure things out on my own, but thankfully I am never on my own and never outside of the reach of God's love. I hope that through the pages of this book God will have whispered the same to you. I hope that he will have breathed courage into your heart, given you a safe place of rest on your journey, and will have encouraged you that no matter how uncertain the future is, he will never change. He is always with you.

Thanks for being part of the journey.

A RESILIENT LIFE

Devotional Readings by Diane Regan

AN INTRODUCTION FROM PATRICK

Good habits really help us become more resilient. When we're under pressure those habits can keep us afloat and stop us from crashing into the rocks. Reading the Bible is one such good habit but I often find I don't know where to start, particularly when I feel under pressure. We hope the following notes will aid you in staying afloat. Diane has written them to explore the topic of resilience with Bible references and verses, thoughts, reflections and prayers. We hope that they will be an accessible and helpful resource for you over the next 27 days, encouraging you to ground some of the principles we've discussed, to reflect further on resilience, and so that you might know how loved you are.

Day 1 A resilient life

Reading: Romans 3:21–24

'and all are justified freely by his grace through the redemption that came by Christ Jesus.' (v24)

Every person, since time began, is completely unique. Not only do we each have our own thumb print and DNA, we all have our own stories; our own journeys. Our lives are made up of our life experiences – the bad as well as the good, the failures as well as the successes.

One of the most comforting things I have learned is that making mistakes is OK. It does not mean we are failures; it means we are human. No matter who we are, where we are from, our age or our education, we will let people down and we will get things wrong – probably even on a daily basis. The Bible is filled with stories of people who messed up, made mistakes and got things wrong. At the same time, however, through God's love and grace, so many of these characters are also celebrated for their good works and deeds, their obedience and most importantly their faith.

We can be extremely grateful that God does not look for our record of successes before he pours out his love for us or chooses to use us. He delights and specialises in turning what the world throws out as waste, into redeemed hope and a positive future. Our loving Father wastes nothing. He wants us to grow and thrive. Despite our past, despite our failures, our wrong choices, our mistakes, his grace is freely available for all of us, releasing us and bringing freedom and hope. It is so freeing to know that we don't need to live perfect lives. All we need to do is bring who we are honestly before God. He does not have to use us, but he chooses to. What an absolute privilege.

FOR PRAYER AND REFLECTION

Lord, thank you for your totally undeserved grace. Help me to understand more the reality of your love and hope. Amen.

Day 2 Resting in the storm

Reading: Psalm 91:1–16

'Whoever dwells in the shelter of the Most High will rest in the shadow of the Almighty.' (v1)

My biggest conclusion about life is this: it's hard, but it's so much harder without God. I honestly do not know how people navigate the journey of life without our heavenly Father. There are so many decisions we have to make, and it can be overwhelming – particularly when we have the freedom to make significant and potentially life-changing decisions. We cannot see the future, but we do have an open invitation for a living relationship with the Most High, the Almighty one, who is the beginning and the end. God's patient and loving guidance is available to us every single day.

Two key words in verse 1 are 'dwell' and 'rest'. In order to achieve the rest, we need first to dwell. To dwell requires time. It is not a quick visit or a flick through the Bible. It is an intentional effort to spend time and consciously remain with Jesus. That doesn't have to mean hiding away in a prayer closet, it means taking Jesus with us through our day – including our decisions. With this comes the 'rest'. Knowing we are not on our own. Having confidence that the Almighty is watching over us and is with us. The closer we are to him, the more we can lean in and rest in him.

Psalm 91 depicts a raging storm, and we know that life can feel this way at times. But we read about the Lord covering us with his wings, rescuing and protecting, and bringing deliverance and salvation. When in the midst of a storm, it can be difficult to remember that God is there, let alone be in a state of rest. The miracle is that God is still with us, fighting our battles with us, regardless of whether we feel it or not.

FOR PRAYER AND REFLECTION

Lord, thank you that your Word promises you are always with me, providing shelter, even in the storms. Help me to remember this and learn to dwell and find rest. Amen.

Day 3 He is in the waiting

Reading: Psalm 27:7–14

'Wait for the Lord; be strong and take heart and wait for the Lord.' (v14)

I remember going forwards for prayer in response to a call to those wanting to give their lives to God's service. I remember having felt frustrated at my lack of service up to that point. The lady praying was so patient and filled with wisdom, and after a few minutes of praying, she had a picture of a horse and cart. Just as a cart attached to a horse, following where the horse leads, this was to be my role. I needed to stop pushing ahead, taking on the role of the horse. That role belongs to Jesus. My role was to stay close, following his lead. This was such a simple picture, yet it made a lot of sense to me.

There have since been many times when it has felt as if the horse is not going anywhere, and I have had to wait. This has been especially hard when I have had a hope or expectation of where the horse might be going. The temptation to push ahead is often difficult. However, he is in the waiting. I am forced to rest, prepare, tune in and focus on the horse, not the destination. As I do this, the destination ceases to be so important, and often it is at this point that we start moving again.

OPTIONAL FURTHER READING

Laurie Short, *Finding Faith in the Dark* (Grand Rapids, MI, USA: Zondervan, 2014)

Day 4 Noticing the little things

Reading: Luke 12:6–8
'Indeed, the very hairs of your head are all numbered.' (v7)

We often have meetings in our home, and inevitably at some point, we're asked where the loo is. On one occasion, someone visited the loo, came back to the lounge, picked up her phone and returned to the loo. She eventually explained how she found our loo inspiring and wanted to take a picture of the beautifully decorated quote we had on the wall, by the American writer Kurt Vonnegut: 'Enjoy the little things in life, for one day you will look back and realise they are the big things.' We spent some time talking about how significant the quote was for her, because she was facing some big challenges.

Naturally, it is easier to notice the big things. Whether good or bad, the big things can take priority. The tallest person, the top achieving children, the most expensive car, the biggest house. On the contrary, God is interested in all things, big and small. Think about the intricate detail he put into designing the beautiful ladybird; the amazing strength and ability he gave to the tiny ants. He even knows how many hairs we have on our head.

Taking time to notice and appreciate the little things helps us to cope with the big things, particularly when life becomes overwhelming. Focusing on a smile from a stranger passing by, a wildflower on the side of the road, the laugh of a toddler playing, your favourite song playing on the radio – noticing these things can help fill our emotional tanks. It is so easy to pass them by. They could be seen as trivial or coincidences. Or they could be appreciated as little drops of heaven, sent by God to help you get through your day.

FOR PRAYER AND REFLECTION
I am grateful, Lord, that you see me. You know everything about me, my needs, hopes and disappointments. You know what I need for today and I choose to trust you. Amen.

Day 5 Looking at the wrong thing

Reading: Matthew 6:25–34

'But seek first his kingdom and his righteousness' (v33)

As I was out walking the dogs recently, I knew I had to navigate a narrow path through stinging nettles. I was so pleased that I had avoided getting stung as I entered the final meadow that I took my eyes off the path. Ouch. I was caught by the tiniest, single nettle. Probably the only one in the meadow. Isn't there a parallel here for life? How many times have I been working hard to navigate through a tricky period in my life, when the most unexpected thing comes along and takes me by surprise? It could be a small thing like a nettle, or it could be something big.

A little while ago, I had a tight deadline to meet and was annoyed that my son hadn't managed to arrange a lift home from football practice. I pulled out of my drive and didn't see the car parked on the side of the road. Bang. I had no excuse. I was looking at the wrong thing.

So how do we make sure we're looking at the right thing? What is the right thing? The good news is, it's not about what we physically look at; it's about the attitude of our heart – what we seek.

Despite these two negative situations, seeing things through God's kingdom eyes changed things. I am now more careful on my walks and have started to notice more of God's creation, and I have changed my diary so that I collect my son and spend that weekly time with him.

Mistakes and accidents do happen. On both of these occasions, I was extremely grateful for sting relief cream, forgiving car owners (and husbands) and insurance companies. God does not always stop bad things from happening, but that doesn't mean he isn't there, going through them with us.

FOR PRAYER AND REFLECTION

Dear Lord, thank you that you are always with me and that you want the best for me, despite how things may appear. Help me to see things as you see them. Amen.

Day 6 Just one thing

Reading: Psalm 27:1–6

'One thing I ask from the Lord... that I may dwell in the house of the Lord all the days of my life' (v4)

We were running an icebreaker activity in one of our Wellbeing Group evenings and asked the question, 'If you were stranded on an island and could have any three things, what would they be?' The group found answering this harder than they expected, but then eventually came up with the ideas of: a fishing rod, a knife and a solar-powered mobile phone (with signal). When pushed to then reduce items down to just one thing, they wanted – yes, you guessed it – the mobile phone.

We are built for connection; it is wired into us as part of our DNA. God designed us this way. David wrote in today's psalm that the one thing he asked for was to be able to dwell with God every day. David desired fellowship and communion with God. Back then, to meet with God, or to be able to 'dwell', you had to physically go to the Tabernacle. This required effort, time and dedication.

Even in Jesus' time, you had to go to the Temple to be with God. Jesus' death and resurrection and the promise of the Holy Spirit means this is no longer a requirement. If we ask him to, God has promised he will be with us all the time.

For the majority of people, mobile phones are important possessions as they connect us to everything. We are tempted to have them with us constantly, often for very valid reasons.

David lived and wrote the Psalms about 1,000 BC, before any technology was ever invented, yet his words still resonate with us today. If dwelling with God all the days of our lives was the one thing we focused on and desired, how different would we be today? How would this change our priorities, fears, plans and hopes?

FOR PRAYER AND REFLECTION

Spend a moment considering what your focus is on today. What does your heart dwell on?

Day 7 Going God's way

Reading: Proverbs 3:1–6
'Trust in the Lord with all your heart and lean not on your own understanding' (v5)

When I was new to faith, everything seemed so obvious and clear: God was the hero who was able to fix anything, and there were mostly happy endings. If it was not a happy ending, there was always a reason to blame things on. As the years and their experiences have gone on, there is now more in my life that I do not understand, and even more that I realise I do not know.

As a new Christian, I expected to need God less as I learned and matured. In reality, however, the opposite is true. As each day passes, I am more reliant on God than ever. I need him more and more every day.

The plan I had for my life came and went many years ago. I am sure this is true for most people! Looking back, I can see how, although God has been constantly with me and I am amazed at how although he does not cause bad things to happen, he uses these times for good. My pain and scars of the past can now help others. God has used my journey to change me, to enable me to listen more, to build my resilience and to soften me up. I have learned that it is not about me, my desires and my dreams (although these are important, and most often God-given). God's plans are far greater than my dreams and desires.

It is not about how clever we are, how much we have in the bank, how big our house, how fast our car. Mother Theresa had nothing, no qualifications or official status, yet ended up being one of the most influential people ever to live. Her simple message was to love without judgment and to find beauty in everyone. Her simple acts of love and kindness have left lasting impact on the world.

FOR PRAYER AND REFLECTION
Lord, your ways are perfect. You are the beginning and the end. Thank you that even though I am just one person in the whole universe, you still choose to use me. Amen.

Day 8 Undeserved good and bad

Reading: James 1:16–18

'Every good and perfect gift is from above, coming down from the Father' (v17)

How often do you hear people, particularly children, say the words 'It's not fair'? Having four children of my own, I have heard it many times. And it's true, life is not fair. Test results do come back with devastating news, marriages do break up, loved ones do pass away, accidents do happen, employees do lose jobs. Many times, it's not fair; it's undeserved.

So what do we deserve? How should it work? Should the positive things that happen in our lives be according to how good we are, how hard we work?

It's helpful here to consider the undeserved good in our lives. Have we had people to love and people who have loved us? Do we have a place to sleep? Do we have enough food for the next meal? Do we have the opportunity to see the sunrise or the sunset? Have we people around us who could help us in time of need? Someone we can call on for prayer? These may be simple things, but they are gifts. I am certain there is so much more in each day you could add to your list of undeserved good.

When I was first taught about the word 'grace', I was given the acronym 'God's Riches At Christ's Expense'. This centres me and reminds me about what Jesus went through on my behalf. His death was the ultimate example of unfairness. So, yes, the undeserved bad happens, and it can often feel as if there is more bad than good, but Jeremiah 17:7 promises, 'blessed is the one who trusts in the LORD'. When we take time to look at our blessings now and in days gone by, we can be filled with joy, knowing that regardless of who we are or what we've done, our loving Father showers us with good and perfect gifts from above.

FOR PRAYER AND REFLECTION

Father, thank you for the undeserved provision you bless me with every day. Please open my eyes to see more of your wonderful work in my life. Amen.

Day 9 Stronger than each storm

Reading: Acts 27:13–25

'keep up your courage... for I have faith in God' (v25)

Today's passage depicts Paul in a boat going through a storm. We're told how the storm was so violent the people on board 'finally gave up all hope of being saved' (v20). They had thrown all excess cargo overboard in order to help keep the boat afloat, meaning that on top of the fear and loss of hope, they were hungry. After many days, at the point of no hope, Paul had a vision of an angel in the night and was told the boat would be destroyed but not one life would be lost. Reading to the end of the chapter, we find out there were 276 people on board. The account is amazing.

A few years ago, Patrick and I felt as if we were in a tiny boat being tossed around by huge waves in the middle of an unknown ocean. We had no idea where we were going; we could not see any direction, either by daylight or stars during the night. We did not even have faith we would safely reach a shore. During this time, we found comfort in the prayer of Saint Brendan: 'I trust You to be stronger than each storm within me. I will trust in the darkness and know that my times, even now, are in Your hand.' Amen to that.

OPTIONAL FURTHER READING

Patrick Regan, *Honesty Over Silence* (Farnham: CWR, 2018)

Day 10 Muscle growth

Reading: 1 Timothy 4:4–8

'For physical training is of some value, but godliness has value for all things' (v8)

Imagine resilience is like a muscle. Firstly, in order for the muscle to grow, it has to break a little. Body builders increase their muscle capacity by exercising, pushing themselves further, lifting heavier and heavier weights. Athletes exercise in a similar way: pushing themselves to run further and faster. It hurts, but this intentional pain increases their ability. The breakage in the fibres of the muscles causes the body to repair the muscle and therefore make it stronger.

In the same way, going through difficult and challenging times in our lives, when we feel broken, has the ability to make us stronger.

Secondly, it is important to note that rest plays a huge role in building up the muscle, in repairing the broken fibres. If the muscle does not have the opportunity to rest, it will not repair and get stronger – it will remain broken. This is also true for resilience.

When we go through a difficult time or when we're in survival mode, we can only continue for so long. We need to recognise when to stop and rest, allowing ourselves to repair and strengthen in order continue. Taking time out can be difficult, but it is vital.

The third thing a muscle needs in order to grow is the right nutrition. Comparing this to ourselves and resilience, healthy eating does of course help, but we also need to healthily feed our mind, spirit and soul. There is little point in exercising and resting well if we then fill ourselves with the wrong things. Today's passage encourages us to live healthily in our spirit and soul too through thanksgiving, and through prayer. What do you think that might look like for you today?

FOR PRAYER AND REFLECTION

Lord, you have the best food for my mind, spirit and soul. Thank you that I can come to you to refresh and rebuild strength into my life. Amen.

Day 11 Bouncing back

Reading: Ephesians 2:4–10

'For we are God's handiwork... to do good works, which God prepared in advance for us to do.' (v10)

I love the fictional character Tigger who features in a lot of Winnie the Pooh stories by A.A. Milne. In the illustrations by Ernest H. Shepard that accompany the stories, Tigger has an exceptionally strong and long tail that he coils like a spring and uses to bounce. He has a wonderfully positive personality, and is always wanting to help and get involved, despite often becoming more of a hindrance than a help. Regardless of how disastrous his contribution may end up being, Tigger always manages to bounce back in a positive way. He is often quoted, 'Life is not about how fast you run or how high you climb but how well you bounce.' On this occasion, I could not agree more with Tigger.

Resilience is often described as bouncing back. But without a long and strong tail, coiled like a spring, how do we do this?

One of the key ways Tigger was able to 'bounce' was by being confident in using his natural gifts and talents. He is famously known for not being able to climb trees, and once he knew this was not his gifting, he was OK with it and stopped trying.

Have we spent time working out what God has prepared in advance for us to do, or are we trying to a job we are not called to do, which requires talents and giftings God has not given us? Let's consider what natural talents and giftings God has given us that will help us to bounce through life. These abilities are his handiwork, personally designed for us. They are our unique tools. Using them hand in hand with God can lead to an exciting adventure. The most important thing is to listen to him and follow his lead.

FOR PRAYER AND REFLECTION

Spend time considering your God-given gifts. If you are not sure of them, start by listing what you enjoy, what you are good at and what others say you are good at.

Day 12 Grit

Reading: Hebrews 12:1–3

'And let us run with perseverance the race marked out for us' (v1)

Angela Duckworth is a contemporary American academic and psychologist who coined the term 'grit' in her study of what enables success. Angela describes grit as 'perseverance and passion for long-term goals', which leads to success.[1]

Yesterday we looked at talents, abilities and giftings, and spent some time considering what our God-given gifts are. Today we are looking at the role of goals in resilience. If we know what we are living for, what we are using our gifts and abilities for, then this helps us to be able to keep going through life's rollercoaster ups and downs.

The pilot of a plane will know the landing destination. However, rarely will the plane's journey be a direct, straight line from the starting point to the landing point. The pilot has to navigate the plane through a whole host of situations, such as other planes in the sky, wind thermals and varied weather conditions.

In the same way, knowing our long-term goal does not mean we can plan our route exactly, but it does give us an idea of the direction we need to go in. We need to be flexible to allow for the ups and downs. Life happens, we will make mistakes and we will face challenges along the way, but having our end goal helps us to get back up and keep going.

As Christians, our overall long-term goal is to worship Jesus and to be a conduit for others to know him. This requires perseverance and, certainly, passion. Our level of focus on this goal determines our level of grit, and impacts every area of our lives. It's good to know that Jesus is with us every step of the way.

FOR PRAYER AND REFLECTION

Spend some time considering your long-term goals in life. Are they realistic and achievable? Do they need refining?

Day 13 Capability

Reading: 1 Peter 5:6–10

*'And the God of all grace... will himself restore you
and make you strong, firm and steadfast.'* (v10)

According to the Royal College of Psychiatrists, we need the
following five things to cope well in life: to accept ourselves and know
what we need; to have caring relationships with people; to have clear
expectations of ourselves and others; to be part of a community; and
to be believed in.

　As Christians, we could rewrite this as: to be honest, vulnerable
and courageous; to love and be loved in a supportive environment;
to live in accordance with God's Word; to be in communion with God,
and in fellowship with other Christians; to be accepted and valued.

　God's plan is not just for us to cope, but to flourish. We cannot do
this on our own, and as Christians it is comforting to know we are not
on our own.

　We need to be honest, vulnerable and courageous. For some of us
this means removing our mask. For some of us it means accepting
where we are and asking for help. Being part of God's family can
bring huge blessing. It is wonderful that in God's kingdom there
is no barrier of race, age, culture or background. We also need to
spend time reading God's Word and in prayer. Through this, we will
know more of the life-changing truth that we are accepted, loved and
valued by our loving Father just as we are.

　Take a moment to think about your own life and prayerfully
consider those two lists of things we need in order to cope well in
life – the list suggested by psychiatrists, and the suggested list for us
as Christians. Although we know we have a loving God who is with
us all the time, is he nudging you to work on an area in your life at the
moment? Are you spending time with him, with others, and accepting
yourself? While it's true that these things require vulnerability, they
allow us to flourish.

FOR PRAYER AND REFLECTION

Thank you, Father, that I am not on my own, that you love me
completely and that you want me to not just cope but flourish and be
all you have made me to be. Amen.

Day 14 Antifragile

Reading: Colossians 1:15–20

'He is before all things, and in him all things hold together.' (v17)

The opposite of resilience is fragility. Nassim Nichoals Taleb, a scholar and former trader and risk analyst, came up with the term 'antifragile' following his work focusing on problems of randomness, probability and uncertainty. He then wrote his book, *Antifragile: Things that Gain from Disorder*. According to Taleb, antifragility is beyond resilience or robustness. The resilient resists or deals with issues but may stay the same; the antifragile focus on the learning that can result of an issue and uses the experience to improve.

The airline industry is a good example of antifragile – every time there is an incident, they open up to other airlines and share all the technical details of what they understand to have happened so that everyone is stronger in the long run. That way, other aircrafts can fix any potential faults. It's why there are incredibly low numbers of incidents on passenger aircraft, despite millions of flights every year.

Practicing antifragility therefore requires honesty and vulnerability – being honest with ourselves and showing vulnerability to others – which is not easy.

The title for today's reading in the NIV is, 'The supremacy of the Son of God'. Jesus is the supreme example of antifragile. He is beyond resilience, outside of time and space. Jesus is beyond perfection. Taleb looked at the benefit drawn out of chaos, and created a new word, yet God was already there before time began. He brought order and beauty out of nothing and created the whole world. What a privilege to be part of his family, that we can call Him Father. In our efforts to become antifragile, let's look to the invincible Jesus.

FOR PRAYER AND REFLECTION

Father, you created the whole universe, yet you call me your child. There is nothing in my life that is too big or too difficult for me to come to you with. Amen.

Day 15 Different types of resilience

Reading: Psalm 46:8–11
'Be still and know that I am God' (v10)

There are many different types of resilience: engineering resilience – improving a product to be stronger; plant resilience – developing to withstand the environment (such as deeper roots in windier places); psychological resilience – the capacity to recover quickly.

This last type, psychological resilience can be broken down even more. A quick Google search can include the following catgories: social, family, community, organisational, cultural, emotional, mental etc.

The three main words from the above list are 'improving', 'developing' and 'recover'. These are all active words, so why do we have in the key verse the instruction to 'be still'? These two words alone are the opposite of action. However, the additional words, 'and know that I am God' are an active challenge that requires knowledge, faith and trust – and these take time to build. This active command requires our commitment to improve, to develop and helps us to recover. Verse 10 is close to the end of a whole psalm about how God is our refuge and strength. As a Christian, understanding what it means to be a child of the Almighty can help us live with resilience.

OPTIONAL FURTHER READING
Tom and Christine Sine, *Living on Purpose* (Grand Rapids, MI, USA: Baker Books, 2002)

Day 16 A life with meaning

Reading: Acts 2:42–47

'They devoted themselves to the apostles' teaching and to fellowship' (v42)

Since the turn of the century, there has been a lot of research into resilience. Until this point, it was generally accepted that it was all to do with genetics: some people were just naturally able to cope with life better than others, although there were useful skills that could be learned to help improve their ability to cope. As part of a recent study, research was carried out to determine if there were common characteristics among those who survived concentration camps, and over the next few days we will take a look at the findings.

The common characteristic was a sense of meaning for their lives. Victor Frankl was a holocaust survivor. During his time in the camp he developed 'meaning therapy', which is explained in his book *Man's Search for Meaning*. For Frankl, meaning came from having purposeful work, love and courage in the face of difficulty.

The most resilient establishment in the world to date is the Church. For over 2,000 years it has existed. It is all over the world and continues to grow. The Church has lasted through wars, corruption, political turmoil, famines and recessions – because it has deep meaning. It exists to bring together believers to worship the living Jesus Christ. It is not dependent on finance, buildings or structure, just the shared goal of worshiping Jesus. What started with one man, Jesus, and his twelve disciples, is now estimated to include over two billion people.

As Christians, despite how difficult life can get, we have meaning that drives us to carry on – with a heritage of 2,000 years and fellowship with two billion other believers.

FOR PRAYER AND REFLECTION

Dear Lord, I am so grateful for all those who have gone before me and those who currently stand with me. Thank you for the privilege of worshipping you. Amen.

Day 17 A life with purpose

Reading: 1 Peter 2:4–10
'But you are a chosen people... that you may declare the praises of God' (v9)

While in Auschwitz, Victor Frankl used his skills as a psychologist to encourage his fellow prisoners and to help them to find not only meaning, but a purpose. Those in the camp who gave up felt they had no purpose, no reason to carry on. Frankl encouraged them to stop looking to understand why they were in the camp, but instead to focus on what they could do while there. To find a purpose that they imposed on themselves, rather than that which was imposed onto them.

During a job interview, I was surprised to hear the question 'What gets you out of bed in the morning?' On most days, I could honestly say it's the dogs needing to be let out and then fed, the kids needing to get to school, the washing machine needing to be put on and me needing to get to work. This was obviously not the answer the interviewer would have wanted. He would have wanted to know what motivated me; the 'why', not 'what' I did. The real answer would therefore have been my love for my family, my passion for my work and my love for Jesus. This is my underlying purpose and this is the real reason I get out of bed.

Our ultimate purpose is to worship Jesus, but this flows into all areas of our life. God wants us to have life and live life to the full (John 10:10). What does this mean? Are we living abundantly? This does not mean that God promises a full bank account, a big house and fast car, it means finding joy and hope, despite our circumstances, in living our lives filled with purpose. It means finding value and purpose in loving, serving and supporting those around us. When life is about living for Jesus, our whole motivation and opportunities to see joy increase.

FOR PRAYER AND REFLECTION

We looked earlier in the devotions at our God-given gifts, and then our goals. Spend some time praying and considering your unique purpose as a result of these gifts and goals.

Day 18 Acceptance

Reading: Psalm 139:1–6

'You have searched me, LORD, and you know me.' (v1)

As part of the research into who survived the concentration camps, it was found that the first group of people who did not survive were those who were optimists. They were fine at the start, believing they would be 'out by Christmas', then 'by this time next year'. This helped their ability to cope in the short term, but, as time progressed, their optimism left – along with their hope – which proved disastrous. Fixing their focus on the hope of leaving the camp, they hadn't accepted the prospect that they may never leave the camp, or at the very least, would be there for a very long time.

Optimism is a great tool to use in the short term, but in order to keep going for the long term, accepting the reality of current situations and circumstances is vital. Although it may be more painful at first, once we have accepted things we are able to keep going longer.

In the same way, although we live with the promise and hope of the wonder of heaven and an eternal life with Jesus, we still need to be able to accept and live in and through whatever life's current challenges and difficulties may be. It helps to know that God is not just our future hope, he is with us in all our situations and circumstances. He knows when we sit and when we rise, he knows our every thought and action, and he will never leave us.

He knows us better than we know ourselves; even the number of hairs on our head. Knowing we can trust him can bring comfort, particularly when we cannot see a way ahead in a difficult time.

FOR PRAYER AND REFLECTION

Dear Father, you know every situation and circumstance in my life. Please give me the strength and grace to accept where I am and to keep my faith and hope. Amen.

Day 19 Contentment

Reading: Philippians 4:10–13
'I have learned to be content whatever the circumstances.' (v11)

Paul wrote his letter to the Philippians while in prison. He wrote about gratitude and contentment, despite his obvious present challenges. In the same way, a common characteristic of those who survived a concentration camp was the ability to find contentment: to find joy, whatever their situation. This may have been by dwelling on a memory of a loved one, watching a bird fly overhead, or noticing a tiny shoot of a plant growing through a crack.

In her book, *The Hiding Place*, Corrie ten Boom details how she was able to practice joy and contentment while in Ravensbrook Concentration Camp. She tells one story of how she and her sister Betsie, despite the most terrible conditions, found joy even from the lice and fleas that swarmed their barracks. The infestation meant the guards wouldn't enter the barracks, and that gave them a certain amount of freedom to read the Bible aloud and pray.

The opposite of contentment is disappointment, sadness, resentment, unrest, frustration, anger and pain. Surely Paul was wise to find the secret to living life well. Contentment meant that he was filled with joy, hope, peace, love and faith despite his unsettling circumstances. If he could find contentment in prison, and Corrie ten Boom could find it in Ravensbrook, then there is every hope that with God's help we too can find contentment whatever our circumstances.

The Bible is filled with instructions to praise God whatever our circumstances (1 Thess. 5:18). No matter what is going on, I have found singing worship songs, or just listening and singing from my heart, dramatically changes everything.

FOR PRAYER AND REFLECTION

Dear Father, I praise you despite my circumstances. I praise you despite my feelings. I thank you for your constant love and help. Amen.

Day 20 Holding on to values

Reading: Philippians 4:4–9
'whatever is true, whatever is noble, whatever is right ... think about such things.' (v8)

In a concentration camp, there was one thing the guards could not take away from a prisoner: their innermost thoughts. No matter what happened, how degraded they were, how cruelly they were treated, they could still have their thoughts and they could still choose to have their values.

In terms of both individuals and organisations, values are the cornerstones. They are the foundations from which we make decisions. Have you ever been in a situation where someone didn't respond to something in the way you expected? It doesn't necessarily mean the way they reacted was wrong; it was just they responded out of a different value system to yours.

Everyone has a value system, even if they've have never taken the time to figure it out. We all have values, and it's quite likely that our friends or people we naturally gravitate towards will probably share a good proportion of them. Today's passage suggests some great values. Skimming through the first half of Philippians 4, we find love, gentleness, thankfulness, peace, honesty, purity, righteousness and excellence.

If we had to reduce the Christian values down to one single core value, it would be love. 1 Corinthians 13 expands this and explains how everything comes out of love. Love is the most powerful word, emotion, value and weapon. We are commanded to love, but it is only because He first loved us and His love is our anchor through the storm. Clinging on to this value of love can help us through life's difficulties.

Do you tend to feel or experience God's love more closely during times of difficulty, or times of ease?

FOR PRAYER AND REFLECTION
Dear Father, thank you for your love. Please fill me with it each day, so that I have strength to carry on and can pass on Your love to those around me. Amen.

Day 21 Growth in the darkness

Reading: Psalm 139:7–12

'the night will shine like the day, for darkness is as light to you.' (v12)

I love the changing seasons and the differences each one brings. In autumn, leaves fall to the ground and the trees may look as though they are dead. However, in the darkness, the fallen leaves are preparing rich soil for new plants and make way for new leaves that have started to form, ready to reveal themselves in the spring.

Darkness is often considered negative, yet consider the stars – although always there, they can only be seen at night. A plant can only live due to the formation of the roots and the growth that takes place in darkness.

Our sight is limited in the dark, so we naturally go towards the light. But if we would allow ourselves to walk in the darkness, our eyes would adjust, and we would see more than we thought possible.

God uses the darkness just as much as the light. He created the darkness. We grow in the darkness. Our bodies recover and refresh in the darkness. So embrace God's glory of creation that is evident in the darkness just as much as the light. Do you have any areas in your life that feel like a struggle in the dark? Take another look: is God using this time for you to grow?

OPTIONAL FURTHER READING

Barbara Brown Taylor, *Learning to Walk in the Dark* (Norwich: Canterbury Press, 2015)

Day 22 A matter of perspective

Reading: 2 Corinthians 4:16–18

'So we fix our eyes not on what is seen, but on what is unseen' (v18)

I was recently running a weekly group, focusing on finding tools for positive mental and emotional wellbeing. One of the most useful tools we found for when struggling with something (large or small) was to take time to look at things from a different perspective.

We imagined we could jump into a helicopter and fly up high. While there, we would look at our situation or circumstance to see if we could find additional bits of information that could help us. We would ask questions like: how did this situation come about? Is there an additional resource or extra support that would help resolve it? Is this part of a bigger picture that, now is seen, makes more sense? Changing perspective, widening the focus and seeing the bigger picture always helps.

During a meeting, I once heard negative words from a member of a committee I lead. As much as we valued his experience and skill, his negativity was unfortunately starting to push the rest of us back, forming stumbling blocks for the wider group. My immediate reaction was to remove his invitation to be part of the committee but, before I did so, with God's help, I 'went up into the helicopter' and looked down. From a different perspective, it became clear to me that he was struggling personally and needed support. My resolve was to privately check in on him. What a turnaround! My attitude completely changed from anger and frustration to concern and love. I thought my asking him was for our benefit, but actually it was for his to be able to receive the support and help that he needed. God's perspective is always the best.

FOR PRAYER AND REFLECTION

Dear Lord, help me to see with your eyes, from your perspective, not only as I deal with my own personal circumstances but also to help those around me. Amen.

Day 23 Practising the presence

Reading: Psalm 16:1–11
'I keep my eyes always on the Lord... I shall not be shaken.' (v8)

In my twenties I learned about Brother Lawrence, a seventeenth-century French monk. Born to disadvantaged parents, to escape poverty he joined the army where he was guaranteed his meals. While there, he experienced God and, following injury, retired and eventually joined a monastery in Paris. Brother Lawrence was given work in the kitchen that was mundane, tedious and repetitive. As he continued his chores of cooking and cleaning, he developed the ability to change his attitude to do all his jobs as if doing them for Jesus. Brother Lawrence turned every act he did into worship: from peeling potatoes, to washing pots, to picking up straw. There was no longer any mundane for him. From that moment on, he did everything out of his love for Jesus; for God's presence. This became known as 'practising the presence of God'.

While learning about Brother Lawrence, we were challenged to find our own simple and mundane moments and change them to become opportunities to practise the presence of God. I chose two things. Every time a phone rings, I allow the first two rings to centre me, to give me a chance to pray for God's presence in my conversation. The second thing is that every time I see a tree, I imagine the stretched-out branches are praising the Lord, and I join in, practising the presence. Other suggestions people came up with were putting dot stickers around their house, car or workplace, so every time they saw them, they were reminded to practise the presence. Since building these triggers into my life, I am grateful they have become firm habits.

FOR PRAYER AND REFLECTION

What two mundane and simple tasks could you turn into habits that prompt you to practise the presence of God?

Day 24 Self-compassion

Reading: 2 Corinthians 1:1–7

'we can comfort those in any trouble with the comfort we ourselves receive from God.' (v4)

What is self-compassion? Let me start by saying what it is not. It is not self-esteem. It is not self-indulgence.

If your best friend was going through a hard time and asked for your help, you wouldn't respond by saying they were silly to get into the situation in the first place, and that they need to toughen up, accept the responsibility and sort it out themselves. But – take a moment here – how often do you talk to yourself that way? We need to demonstrate to ourselves that same compassion we show to others.

So, what is self-compassion? What does it look like? Self-compassion means not constantly blaming yourself and putting yourself down for things that have happened outside of your control. Self-compassion means not putting yourself under the pressure of totally unrealistic expectations.

It is treating yourself the way you would your best friend. It is allowing yourself to be loved for who you are, with all your flaws and imperfections, flowing from the love you receive from your loving Father God.

How is this related to resilience? The ability to cope with life can be influenced by what determines our sense of success or failure in the first place. If we set the standard too high, then we are more likely to fall. Practising self-compassion and kindness to ourselves helps to remove the unhelpful self-judgment of unrealistic expectations and standards, and as a result we will not feel the need to bounce back so many times.

As you reflect on this today, is God bringing to mind any particular areas in your own life where you could show yourself some more compassion?

FOR PRAYER AND REFLECTION

Father, please forgive me for the lack of compassion I have given myself. Thank you that through your love and kindness, I have all I need to keep going. Amen.

Day 25 Gratitude

Reading: 1 Thessalonians 5:12–28
*'give thanks in all circumstances; for this is God's will for you
in Christ Jesus.'* (v18)

One thing I really dislike is whinging. But I was told that if a child whinges, it doesn't mean they aren't grateful (although they may be too young understand gratitude); it is generally a response to the feeling they are not being heard. Once I learned this, I could find solutions, and I was enormously grateful as these stopped the whinging.

Gratitude plays a huge part in being able to build resilience in our lives. The Harvard Mental Health Letter, first published in November 2011,[2] reports back on the research carried out by psychologists on two groups. One group was asked to write daily notes of gratitude, while another group was asked to note their irritations. Those who practised gratitude were more healthy and happy. They exercised more, had stronger relationships and generally better outlooks on life.

For some people, being grateful is not something that comes naturally. However, there are ways to build gratitude into your life. An easy step to start with is to begin a gratitude journal. At the end of the day, write down three things you are grateful for. This may be hard to think of at first, but as each day passes, you will notice more and more. Another thing you can do is consciously thank people for what they do, however small. This not only benefits you, but they will feel valued and appreciated.

Prayer is also another opportunity to thank God for all that he has done in your life. In challenging ourselves to be thankful to God, we are drawn into gratitude, taking more notice of his extraordinary goodness to us.

FOR PRAYER AND REFLECTION

Father, I am so grateful for all you do for me. Please forgive me for the times when when I don't notice the many things you do. Please help me see more of your love. Amen.

Day 26 Strength to carry on

Reading: Psalm 46:1–7
'God is our refuge and strength, an ever-present help in trouble.' (v1)

I hope you've found these readings helpful as we've looked together at a few more aspects of resilience. We know that making mistakes does not make us a failure, it makes us human. We have discovered that God is there in the waiting, in the little simple parts of our lives, wanting us to keep our eyes on him as his ways are perfect. We have looked at the ability to keep going, to be able to bounce back, to have grit, to develop and grow, to learn to rest and to look after ourselves. We have taken time to look at our God-given gifts, our goals, our life's purpose and ways of practising gratitude. We have delved into research on how people kept going through some of history's toughest times. We have considered Brother Lawrence and explored ways we too can practise the presence of God.

All the way through the month, we have seen, day after day, that God is faithful. God is close to us; he will never leave us. We began the month exploring how we have the invitation to dwell in the shelter of the most high. Today our key verse reminds us that God is our refuge and strength.

I am reminded of the story of Elijah who, despite his amazing victory over the prophets of Baal, still needed a place of refuge in which to build up his strength.

We are all in need, regardless of our position, age, status or experience. Yet at the same time, we can all help. Working together and looking out for one another is one of the joys of being a Christian. Called to be in fellowship, we need one another. So reach out. Encourage your fellow believers today. You're all doing a great job, even though it may not feel like it. You know how the story ends. Keep going. You've got this.

FOR PRAYER AND REFLECTION

Dear Lord, please speak to me and show me ways I can encourage others in times of difficulty. Help me to direct people to your refuge and strength. Amen.

Day 27 There is always hope

Reading: Romans 15:1–13

'May the God of hope fill you with all joy and peace as you trust in him'
(v13)

When my husband was going through a tough time, we thought it
would be a good idea to get him a dog. Not only would it be good
company for him, it would encourage him to spend time outside and
give him something else to focus on. A few weeks later, our little
bundle of fur arrived, and we chose the name Hope, as a positive
affirmation for our household. It didn't take long for us to realise
the error in the name we chose. Our neighbours must have thought
something was very wrong when over the next few weeks we
shouted out, 'No Hope!' There would even occasionally have heard
us say, 'We've lost Hope.'

Joking aside, 'hope' is the last word relating to resilience that
we are going to look at. Hope is saying that everything passes and
tough times don't last forever. It is remembering that although we
go through storms, difficult situations and circumstances, we have a
promised future in Jesus. We have assurance and hope that he will
come again, that he will restore all things and create a new heaven
and earth. With God, everything is possible. With God, there is always
hope.

OPTIONAL FURTHER REFLECTION

Is there someone you know who needs encouragement today, to
know that everything passes, nothing lasts forever?

These devotional readings have also been published in Waverley Abbey
Resources' Bible reading notes. To find out more about the Bible reading
notes available, visit **waverleyabbeyresources.org/free-bible-reading-notes**

ENDNOTES

Introduction
[1] Chris Johnstone, *Seven Ways to Build Resilience* (London: Robinson, 2019) p20.
[2] https://hbr.org/2002/05/how-resilience-works (accessed 16 November 2020).
[3] K.J. Ramsey, *This Too Shall Last* (Grand Rapids, MI: Zondervan, 2020) p95.

Chapter 1
[1] Dalai Lama, Desmond Tutu and Douglas Abrams, *The Book of Joy: Lasting Happiness in a Changing World* (London: Hutchinson, 2016), pp223, 225.
[2] Liz Carter, *Catching Contentment: How To Be Holy Satisfied* (London: IVP, 2018), pp35–36.
[3] https://youtu.be/GvWWO7F9kQY (accessed 19 June 2020). Also drawn from https://youtu.be/FpgLAuZdutM (accessed 19 June 2020).
[4] www.psychologytoday.com/gb/therapy-types/acceptance-and-commitment-therapy (accessed 24 June 2020).
[5] https://youtu.be/VYht-guymF4 (accessed 9 November 2020).
[6] Psychologies Magazine, *Real Strength* (Yalding, UK: Kelsey Publishing, 2017) p167.

Chapter 2
[1] Tom Rath and Jim Harter, *Wellbeing* (New York: Gallup Press, 2010).
[2] Vaillant study, https://en.wikipedia.org/wiki/Grant_Study (accessed 16 November 2020).
[3] https://www.azquotes.com/quote/850026 (accessed 1 July 2020).
[4] https://relevantmagazine.com/faith/stop-taking-jeremiah-2911-out-context/ (accessed 10 November 2020).
[5] https://www.moralstories.org/the-cracked-pot/ (accessed 1 July 2020).
[6] https://www.gooder.me.uk/on-being-imperfect/ (accessed 1 July 2020).
[7] Henri Nouwen, *The Wounded Healer*, https://henrinouwen.org/meditation/the-wounded-healer/ (accessed 10 November 2020).
[8] https://brenebrown.com/blog/2015/06/18/own-our-history-change-the-story/ (accessed 9 November 2020).
[9] Brené Brown, *Braving the Wilderness* (London: Random House, 2017) p157.
[10] Brené Brown, *Braving the Wilderness*, p160.
[11] Mark Manson, *The Subtle Art of Not Giving a F*ck* (USA: Harper One, 2016) p56.
[12] C.S. Lewis, quoted at http://www.quotationspage.com/quote/25736.html.

[13]Michelle Obama, *Becoming* (New York: Viking, 2018) p421.
[14]Steve and Chris Hepden, *What Christians Should Know About Their Value to God* (Lancaster: Sovereign World Limited, 1999) p25.

Chapter 3
[1]Sheryl Sandberg and Adam Grant, *Option B* (UK: WH Allen, 2017) p16.
[2]https://www.nytimes.com/2020/06/18/health/resilience-relationships-trauma.html (accessed 10 July 2020).
[3]Sheryl Sandberg and Adam Grant, *Option B*, p22.
[4]Gregory A. Boyd, *Benefit of the Doubt* (Ada, MI: Baker Books, 2013) p76.
[5]www.optimize.me/quotes/carol-dweck/111492-the-passion-for-stretching-yourself-and-sticking-to-it-even (accessed 10 November 2020).
[6]Viktor Frankl, *Man's Search For Meaning* (London: Rider Books, 2004).
[7]https://www.ted.com/talks/susan_david_the_gift_and_power_of_emotional_courage#t-933098 (accessed 10 July 2020).
[8]Susan David, *Emotional Agility* (Great Britain: Penguin, 2017) p77.
[9]Bryan Stevenson, *Just Mercy* (London: Scribe Publications, 2015) p289.
[10]Bryan Stevenson, *Just Mercy*, p290.
[11]Bryan Stevenson, Just Mercy, p290.

Chapter 4
[1]Malcolm Duncan, *Good Grief* (Oxford: Lion Hudson, 2020) p250.
[2]https://tanyamarlow.com/tbn-patrick-regan-2020/ (accessed 22 July 2020).
[3]https://psychcentral.com/blog/coping-with-grief-the-ball-the-box/ (accessed 22 July 2020).
[4]https://www.apa.org/news/apa/2020/04/grief-covid-19 (accessed 16 July 2020).
[5]C.S. Lewis, *A Grief Observed* (London: Faber & Faber) pp5–6.
[6]https://tanyamarlow.com/kay-and-rick-warren-on-suffering-and-grief-quotes/ (accessed 9 November 2020).
[7]Daniel J. Simundson, 'suffering' in *Anchor Yale Bible Dictionary*, ed David Noel Freedman and Gary A. Herion (New Haven, CT: Yale University Press, 1992), 6:222.
[8]Kathleen O'Connor, *Lamentations and the Tears of the World* (Maryknoll, NY: Orbis, 2002) p14, cited in Jeanette Mathews, *Framing Lament* (Eugene, OR: Wipf & Stock Publishers, 2013) p193.

Chapter 5
[1]https://www.traumainformedchurches.org/what-is-trauma (accessed 23 July 2020).
[2]https://www.traumainformedchurches.org/what-is-trauma (accessed 23 July 2020).
[3]Bessel van der Kolk, *The Body Keeps The Score: Mind, Brain and Body in*

the *Transformation of Trauma* (London: Penguin, 2015).

[4]Those with four or more ACES are: two times more likely to have a poor diet; three times more likely to smoke; five times more likely to have had sex under 16 years; two times more likely to binge drink; seven times more likely to have involved in recent violence; 11 times more likely to have been incarcerated; 11 times more likely to have used heroin or crack cocaine. In addition, 64% of those involved in substance misuse and 50% of homeless people have four ACEs or more. Public Health Scotland research: http://www.healthscotland.scot/population-groups/children/adverse-childhood-experiences-aces/overview-of-aces (accessed 24 July 2020).

[5]https://issuu.com/acesupporthub/docs/inspiration_from_ace_interrupters_in_gb/1?ff (accessed 28 July 2020).

[6]I've drawn on a number of resources that you might want to explore for yourself if you're interested in understanding more about trauma: https://fivebooks.com/best-books/psychological-trauma-matthew-green/; https://www.youtube.com/watch?v=53RX2ESIqsM; https://www.youtube.com/watch?v=jFdn9479U3s.

[7]To find out more about the project in Trenchtown, visit www.kintsugihope/projects.

[8]Stephen Joseph and Lisa Butler, 'Positive Changes Following Adversity', *PTSD Research Quarterly*, 21/3, January 2010, quoted in https://trauma-recovery.ca/resiliency/post-traumatic-growth/ (accessed 28 July 2020).

[9]Psychologies Magazine, *Real Strength* (Yalding, UK: Kelsey Publishing, 2017) p16.

[10]https://www.webmd.com/a-to-z-guides/hematidrosis-hematohidrosis#1 (accessed 28 July 2020).

[11]N.T. Wright, *The Day the Revolution Began* (London: SPCK Publishing, 2016) p54.

[12]Rowan Williams, *Being Disciples* (London: SPCK Publishing, 2016) p47.

[13]K.J. Ramsey, *This Too Shall Last* (Grand Rapids, MI: Zondervan, 2020) p156.

Chapter 6

[1]K.J. Ramsey, *This Too Shall Last* (Grand Rapids, MI: Zondervan, 2020) p156.

[2]Tedeschi and Calhoun, 2004, quoted in https://trauma-recovery.ca/resiliency/post-traumatic-growth/ (accessed 16 November 2020).

[3]Chris Johnstone, *Seven Ways to Build Resilience* (London: Robinson, 2019) p286.

[4]You can read more about the David Idowu Foundation at www.davididowufoundation.org.uk.

[5]Woodward and Joseph, 2003, quoted in https://trauma-recovery.ca/resiliency/post-traumatic-growth/.

[6]Sheridan Voysey, *The Making of Us* (Nashville, TN: Thomas Nelson, 2019) p130.

[7]https://angeladuckworth.com/qa/ (accessed 7 August 2020).
[8]https://hbr.org/2002/05/how-resilience-works (accessed 7 August 2020).
[9]https://www.goodreads.com/quotes/137-he-who-has-a-why-to-live-for-can-bear (accessed 10 November 2020).
[10]https://www.joniandfriends.org/about/what-we-do/ (accessed 21 August 2020).
[11]https://www.youtube.com/watch?v=VVXJ8GyLgt0 (accessed 21 August 2020).
[12]K.J. Ramsey, *This Too Shall Last* (Grand Rapids, MI: Zondervan, 2020), p121.
[13]Liggy Webb, Psychologies Magazine, *Real Strength* (Yalding, UK: Kelsey Publishing, 2017) p13.

Chapter 7

[1]Chris Ledger and Wendy Bray, *Insight into Perfectionism* (Farnham, UK: CWR, 2009) p27.
[2]Brené Brown, *Daring Greatly* (New York: Gotham Books, 2012) p129.
[3]Sheila Walsh, *It's Okay Not to Be Okay* (Ada, MI: Baker Books, 2018) p96.
[4]Chris Ledger and Wendy Bray, *Insight into Perfectionism* (Farnham, UK: CWR, 2009) p21.
[5]https://quotes.pub/q/be-still-and-know-that-i-am-god-i-know-i-sometimes-do-countl-400802 (accessed 25 August 2020).
[6]Viktor Frankl quoted in *Resilient* by Rick Hanson (London: Rider Books, 2018) p80.
[7]Susan David, *Emotional Agility* (Great Britain: Penguin, 2016) p13.
[8]www.mindtools.com/pages/article/newTED_85.htm (accessed 28 August 2020).
[9]Mark Manson, *The Subtle Art of Not Giving a F*ck* (USA: Harper One, 2016) p87.
[10]Susan David, *Emotional Agility* (Great Britain: Penguin, 2016) p130.

Liz's Story

[1]If you want to read more of Liz's story, she blogs at www.greatadventure.carterclan.me.uk

Chapter 8

[1]DiSalvo, *Scientific American*, 2017, quoted in https://www.psychologytoday.com/gb/blog/pieces-mind/201712/the-importance-kindness (accessed 26 August 2020).
[2]https://www.goodreads.com/quotes/441565-in-spite-of-everything-i-still-believe-that-people-are (accessed 10 November 2020).
[3]https://www.goodreads.com/quotes/573911-i-think-probably-kindness-is-my-number-one-attribute-in (accessed 10 November 2020).
[4]Christine Carter, 'What We Get When We Give', https://greatergood.

berkeley.edu/article/item/what_we_get_when_we_give (accessed 16 November 2020).

[5]Matt. 9:36; 14:14; 15:32; 20:34; Mark 1:41 (NKJV); 6:34; 8:2; Luke 15:20.
[6]https://upliftconnect.com/hold-space/ (accessed 26 August 2020).
[7]Matt Haig, *Reasons to Stay Alive* (Great Britain: Canongate, 2016) p126.
[8]Kate Bowler, *Everything Happens for a Reason and Other Lies I've Loved* (London: SPCK, 2018) pp173–175.
[9]Daniel J. Siegel, *Mindsight* (London: Oneworld Publications, 2011) p10.
[10]K.J. Ramsey, *This Too Shall Last* (Grand Rapids, MI: Zondervan, 2020) p170.
[11]Debbie Duncan, *The Art of Daily Resilience* (Oxford: Monarch, 2017) p122.
[12]Michael A. Cohn, Barbara L. Fredrickson, Stephanie L. Brown, Joseph A. Mikels, Anne Conway, 'Happiness Unpacked: Positive Emotions Increase Life Satisfaction by Building Resilience', *Emotion*, 9(3), 2009, pp361–368.
[13]Susan David, *Emotional Agility* (Penguin, 2017) p65.
[14]John Mark Comer, *The Ruthless Elimination of Hurry* (London: Hodder & Stoughton, 2019) p64.
[15]http://thunderbirdleadership.com/2017/05/02/compassionate-people-best-boundaries (Accessed January 2021)
[16]https://chapel-archives.oit.duke.edu/documents/sermons/July11WhatMustIDotoInheritEternalLife.pdf (accessed 26 August 2020).
[17]www.ldsliving.com/7-Reasons-We-Reject-Help-and-Kindness-How-That-Hurts-Our-Eternal-Progression/s/90213 (accessed 26 August 2020).

Chapter 9

[1]https://gratefulness.org/resource/its-all-about-the-glass/ (accessed 3 September 2020).
[2]Henri Nouwen, *You Are Beloved* (London: Hodder & Stoughton, 2017) p202.
[3]Karen Reivich and Andrew Shatté, *The Resilience Factor* (Danvers, MA: Broadway Books, 2002) p125 and www.todaysparent.com/family/parenting/how-to-raise-an-optimistic-child/ (accessed 16 November 2020).
[4]https://youtu.be/JMd1CcGZYwU (accessed 3 September 2020).
[5]https://youtu.be/aRV8AhCntXc (accessed 3 September 2020).
[6]https://globalleadership.org/articles/leading-yourself/brene-brown-on-joy-and-gratitude (Accessed January 2021)
[7]https://www.spiritualityandpractice.com/book-reviews/excerpts/view/14100/gratefulness-the-heart-of-prayer (Accessed January 2021)
[8]Will van der Hart and Rob Waller, *The Perfectionism Book* (London: IVP, 2016) p121.
[9]Henri Nouwen, *You are Beloved: Daily Meditations for Spiritual Living* (London: Hodder & Stoughton, 2017), p201.

[10]Tom Wright, *Paul: A Biography* (London: SPCK, 2018) p182.
[11]https://biblehub.com/commentaries/acts/16-24.htm (accessed 3 September 2020).
[12]https://www.goodreads.com/quotes/397119-and-when-i-give-thanks-for-the-seemingly-microscopic-i (accessed 10 November 2020).
[13]Tony Horsfall and Debbie Hawker, *Resilience in Life and Faith* (Abingdon, UK: BRF) p44.
[14]Joshua Choonmin Kang, *Spirituality of Gratitude* (Downers Grove, IL: IVP, 2015) p53.
[15]John Mark Comer, *The Ruthless Elimination of Hurry* (London: Hodder & Stoughton, 2019) p36.

Chapter 10
[1]Chris Johnstone, *Seven Ways to Build Resilience* (London: Robinson, 2019) p47.
[2]Cathy Madavan, *Irresistible* (London: SPCK, 2020) p81.
[3]Henry Cloud, *Necessary Endings* (New York: Harper Business, 2011), https://www.spiritualityandpractice.com/books/reviews/excerpts/view/20787 (accessed 9 September 2020).
[4]Will van der Hart and Rob Waller, *The Power of Belonging* (Colorado Springs, CO: David C Cook 2019) p27.
[5]Donald Capps, *The Depleted Self* (Minneapolis, MN: Fortress Press, 1993) p35.
[6]Heather Churchill and Clare Musters, *Insight Into Shame* (Farnham, UK: CWR, 2019) p37.
[7]https://youtu.be/F0SWMICwtm0 (accessed 9 September 2020).
[8]https://blog.churchsource.com/leaders-heres-one-powerful-way-to-face-your-shadow/ (accessed 9 September 2020).
[9]Greg Boyd, *Seeing is Believing* (Ada, MI: Baker Books, 2004) p36.
[10]Trevor Partridge, *Love With Skin On* (Farnham, UK: CWR, 2016) p87.
[11]Ann Voskamp, *The Broken Way* (Grand Rapids, MI: Zondervan, 2016) p177.
[12]With thanks to Jane Smith for allowing us to reproduce this poem.

A Resilient Life – Devotional Readings by Diane Regan
[1]To read more, search online for Angela Duckworth's article, 'Grit: Perseverance and passion for long-term goals'.
[2]To find out more, visit health.harvard.edu

ABOUT THE AUTHOR

Patrick is CEO and co-founder of Kintsugi Hope, which came about following a series of personal trials and ill-health affecting Patrick and his family. Prior to that, Patrick led urban youth work charity XLP, which he founded in 1996 and ran for 22 years.

Patrick has travelled to over 40 countries, working with and on behalf of the poorest communities, and is a regular contributor on radio and TV on issues of justice and wellbeing. He has received the Mayor of London Peace Award and was also awarded an OBE from Her Majesty the Queen for services to young people. Patrick is an Honorary Fellow of the South Bank University for his contribution towards justice and wellbeing.

Patrick is a passionate communicator equally at home on the main stage at major UK political party conferences and engaging in robust debates in the media as he is connecting with business and community leaders, and speaking to inmates in a maximum security prison or gang leaders in Jamaica. Patrick is also Patron of Welcome Churches, whose vision is for every refugee in the UK to be welcomed by their local church.

Patrick is married to Diane and has four children. He is the author of six books.

Liza Hoeksma works in communications for Soul Survivor Watford church, as well as being a freelance writer and editor. She has written six books with Patrick and collaborated with others such as Mike Pilavachi and Ali Martin from Soul Survivor, Spring Harvest, and Tich & Joan Smith from LIV Village in South Africa.

Discovering
treasure
in life's scars

ABOUT KINTSUGI HOPE

Kintsugi Hope is a charity founded by Patrick and Diane Regan which longs to bring a message of hope for all those struggling and an assurance that it's OK to acknowledge that you are not OK.

Kintsugi Hope trains churches to run Wellbeing Groups in their communities and online. These groups provide safe and supportive spaces for those who are finding life overwhelming. They are places where people who struggle with mental and emotional health challenges are not only accepted and understood, but are given the tools to grow and flourish in community with others.

The aim of these groups, working through local churches, is to foster an attitude of humility – not to judge, fix or rescue, but to be alongside and love one another. Groups will journey together to look at being honest with each other, how to understand and handle our emotions, building healthy relationships and growing in resilience.

To find out more about the work of Kintsugi Hope and the Wellbeing Groups, visit kintsugihope.com

KINTSUGI HOPE AND WAVERLEY ABBEY TRUST PRESENT

BOUNCING FORWARDS

TOUR

NOTES ON RESILIENCE, COURAGE AND CHANGE

Bouncing Forward is an evening of live music and talks.

Many of us know all too well that when we've suffered we don't simply 'bounce back'; difficulties can leave us scarred and changed. But as we face our past and our present with courage and show ourselves kindness and compassion, we find that we can move forwards and discover the truth of God's treasures in our darkness.

With **PATRICK REGAN**

BOOKING NOW

For an application form pls contact **Admin@Kintsugihope.com**

Limited Spaces, due to high demand

Venues need to be in line with Government Covid19 Guidelines

Handling issues that are feared, ignored or misunderstood

An insight into addiction

An insight into anxiety

An insight into bereavement

An insight into anger

An insight into self-esteem

An insight into depression

An insight into burnout

An insight into perfectionism

An insight into self-acceptance

Insight Books

Providing comprehensive and practical insights, the Waverley Abbey Insight Series is based on the Insight teaching days.

Some Insight books are also available in eBook format.

More from Patrick Regan

This journal is designed to give you space to process your thoughts and reflect on whatever's going on in your life and faith, with quotes and Bible verses to inspire you as you write. Produced in partnership with Kintsugi Hope.

Also available: Honesty Over Silence

Honesty Over Silence seeks to break the stigma around mental health and encourage open conversations that bring both understanding and hope. Powerful true stories from Patrick Regan and others about some of life's hardest challenges show how the strength in sharing honestly helps us to grow into the people God created us to be.

Based on the book, the five-session DVD includes interviews and discussion starters, making it ideal for use in small groups.

WAVERLEY ABBEY RESOURCES

in partnership with

kintsugi HOPE

waverleyabbeyresources.org
kintsugihope.com

WAVERLEY ABBEY TRUST

COLLEGE

RESOURCES

HOUSE

waverleyabbeycollege.ac.uk   waverleyabbeyresources.org   waverleyabbeyhouse.org

We are a charity serving Christians around the world with practical resources and teaching. We support you to grow in your Christian faith, understand the times in which we live, and serve God in every sphere of life.

Find a counsellor

WAVERLEY ABBEY
COLLEGE

Many people, at some point in their lives, benefit from professional counselling. If you know someone who is hurting, or you yourself feel that you need help finding a way forward in life, and would like to consider the support of a trained professional, our online Find a Counsellor directory is available to all.

We have seen over 250 students graduate, having studied counselling within a Christian framework, and many have gone on to set up their own counselling practice.

The counsellors listed on our directory are members of, or accredited by, a professional body, and are previous students of the college.

We hope that you find this service helpful.

waverleyabbeycollege.ac.uk/find-a-counsellor-map/